JOHN PAUL II
in the service of love

Text by
Kathryn Spink

Designed and Produced by
Ted Smart & David Gibbon

COLOUR LIBRARY INTERNATIONAL

With St. Paul we repeat: "For the love of Christ restraineth us". Right from the beginning we wish to see our ministry as a service of love; this will permeate all our actions.

Address *Urbi et Orbi* given at the end of the conclave. 17th October, 1978.

Christ, allow me to be and remain a servant of your unique power, a servant of your power who is filled with gentleness, a servant of your endless power, or rather, a servant of your servants.

Homily on the official inauguration in St. Peter's Square. 22nd October, 1978.

IN the silent hours of the night of the 28th September 1978 the thirty-three day pontificate of John Paul I, the "smiling pope", came abruptly if peacefully to its conclusion. High above St. Peter's Square the light in the papal apartment was shining, but unbeknown to the world, the See of Peter was vacant, Rome was without its bishop and the Roman Catholic Church was without a Head. It was not until 5.30 am when Father John Magee, private secretary to the pope, concerned at the failure of John Paul I to appear promptly for Mass, went to the pope's bedroom, that the tragedy was discovered. The man who had appeared so strikingly alive during the previous day's public audience and address to the bishops of the Philippines was found dead in bed, a copy of à Kempis' "Imitation of Christ" open by the bedside. A doctor was called and it was concluded that death of acute coronary thrombosis must have occurred at approximately 11 pm the previous night and so, sadly, the man who had loved people had died alone without the sacraments of the Church. At 10 pm, whilst preparing for bed, he had been given the news of the murder of a left-wing youth in Rome and had sighed, wistfully "Even young people are killing each other now." These were his last recorded words.

As the news of John Paul I's death spread, the world received it with uncomprehending shock. The death of Pope Paul VI on 6th August of the same year had been a sad blow but it had not been altogether unexpected. He himself had remarked to pilgrims at Castelgandolfo as early as 1970 "The clock of time moves inexorably forwards and it points to a forthcoming end" and when the end finally came he had had fifteen years to make an indelible mark upon the papacy. Pope John Paul I's reign on the other hand, had appeared like a promise of hope cut cruelly short before it had time to come to fruition. His homilies had promised a pontificate in continuity with his predecessors – extending back as far as Pius XI. In particular he had claimed "the pastoral plan of Pope Paul VI, our immediate predecessor, has most of all left a strong impression on our heart and in our memory". Yet in the short time that he was granted as pope the man who had once confided "I am only a poor man, accustomed to small things and silence" had brought a new look to the papacy. His refusal to be crowned with the triple-tiered papal tiara as a symbol of regal power, which he saw as wholly unsuited to the "servant of the servants of God", indeed his rejection of any concept of 'coronation' or 'enthronement' was not simply a demonstration of humility, but a definite statement about the Petrine office itself. The ceremony by which he became pope was not a coronation but "the inauguration of his ministry as supreme pastor", a ministry which promised to be one of transparent compassion and honesty of a kind likely to erode some of the barriers of conservatism surrounding the Vatican. While, therefore, his body lay in state in the Sala Clementina and subsequently in St. Peter's, there were few among the endless stream of mourners who came to pay their last respects who did not note with sadness that his red shoes showed so little sign of wear.

Within the Vatican the death of a pope is the starting point for a complex sequence of traditions for which grief, however great, must be temporarily set aside. On the death of John Paul I, the French-born Vatican Secretary of State, Cardinal Jean Villot, became *Camerlengo*, or administrator of the Holy See, a position he would hold until a new successor to Peter had been elected. For the second time in so brief a period the rituals must be observed. The dead pope's forehead must be tapped three times with a silver hammer, his name called and the question posed; "Are you dead?". Once more the seal in the Ring of the Fisherman, engraved with an image of St. Peter in a boat, fishing, a symbol of papal power, must be shattered with a hammer. Every coin new-minted in the Vatican City and every stamp issued must bear the words *sede vacante* and the Vatican newspaper must carry the same imprint indicating that the throne of Peter is un-occupied. Even the uniform of the Swiss Guards must be changed to the dark blue color of mourning.

The same grief was no doubt aggravated by anxiety at the strain on Vatican coffers. Each time a pope dies, and again when a new Pope is elected, a bonus is paid to all Vatican dependants from cardinals to street cleaners (one of John Paul I's less popular acts was to cut the instalment paid on his election by half). Then there are the arrangements and expenses directly involved in the holding of a conclave; the cost of fares and organization of accommodation for many of the 111 conclavists who cannot afford to pay themselves, as well as the expense of preparing the Sistine Chapel, the papal apartments and the robes. Considerations of this kind inevitably create anxieties on a purely practical level but even more serious on this occasion were the implications to the Church as a whole, of the necessity to search once more for a man capable of bearing the onerous office of pope. As one cardinal later remarked: "A mourning on top of another mourning – it is a very grave trial for the Church and we must truly pray. Who knows what awaits us now?" The role of pope, by virtue of its very basis, can be no easy one. The three-fold scriptural foundation of the office as successor of St. Peter: the pope is the rock-apostle upon which the Church of Christ is built (Matthew 16:18-19); he is commanded to "confirm the brethren" (Luke 22:32); and to feed the sheep and the lambs of his flock as a witness of love (John 21:15-17), imposes upon one man an almost intolerable burden of responsibility and authority. Despite the fact that John Paul I abandoned all the titles that theologians had condemned as unscriptural in favor of "pope, bishop of Rome, supreme pastor", the full range of titles traditionally associated with the office:

Bishop of Rome
Vicar of Jesus Christ
Successor of the Prince of the Apostles
Supreme Pontiff of the Universal Church
Patriarch of the West
Primate of Italy
Archbishop and Metropolitan of the Province of Rome
Sovereign of the Vatican State

gives some indication of what is involved. The ruling of Vatican City, an independent and sovereign state with its own yellow and white flag, is in itself no small task. Something in the region of three thousand people are employed within the Vatican walls, although not all of these are citizens. Citizens are not born to the status, but are created because of the work in which they are currently or were once engaged. Cardinals resident in Rome, whether employed or not, automatically join the ranks of citizens which also include the Swiss Guards and all active members of the papal diplomatic corps. The actual administration of this small but vital state, which despite the fact that its nearest water is the rather dubious Tiber, is actually entitled to its own fleet, is undertaken by the Cardinal Secretary of State assisted by a cardinal pro-president and a commission of cardinals. Nevertheless the ultimate responsibility for the Vatican City and its contents rests with the pope, and popes have in general taken this responsibility seriously. This can be but a small task, however, by comparison with that of being leader of the estimated 700 million Roman Catholics in the world. As leader of the Roman Catholic Church, the pope must not only establish and maintain relationships with Church hierarchy throughout the world but must also walk the tightrope of international diplomacy, and be capable of arguing convincingly, but patiently, the position of the Church in an often antagonistic world of science and politics. Furthermore he must maintain harmony between radicals and conservatives within the Roman Catholic Church itself – all this too must be undertaken in the knowledge that when speaking *ex cathedra* on matters of faith and morals he will be regarded within the Roman Catholic Church as speaking with the voice of God Himself and therefore, with infallibility. It is a task which has created in many a supreme sense of isolation. The Lateran Treaty of 1939, between the Italian government and the Church, may have allowed the pope to move outside the confines of the Vatican City but he was still restricted by the necessity for prearrangement. John XXIII's chauffeur, Guido Gusso, recounted how the Holy Father delighted in failing to give the requisite two hours' notice of his intention to go out to the *carabinieri* so that he, like everyone else, could stop at the red traffic lights and wave and bless his people. John XXIII did much to break down the barriers of formality which existed between the pope and even his closest aides. He abolished the custom of always eating alone on the grounds that there was no scriptural foundation for it and rejected the kind of exaggerated ceremony which had meant that in the time of Pius XII officials knelt even when speaking to the pope on the telephone. As Lawrence Elliott writes in his book "I will be called John", ". . . it ran counter to his Bergamesque sense of brotherhood and he was continually ordering people to their feet. When an aged reporter from *L'Osservatore Romano* assured him that he was perfectly comfortable conducting an interview from his knees, John threatened to leave the room unless the man sat in a chair." Despite such progressive steps, however, when John Paul I became pope there still remained enough ritual to make him lonely, so much so that he resorted to telephoning the mother superiors of religious orders for a chat.

The cardinals who assembled in Rome in October for the second conclave of that year were all too aware of what strength, both spiritual and physical, was required of a future pope. Significantly, the man who was to become John Paul II, then Cardinal Wojtyla, had welcomed the election of John Paul I with the words: "Certainly he who has taken on his shoulders the mission of Peter – pastoral responsibility for the entire church – has also taken on his shoulders a heavy cross. We wish to be with him from the beginning of his road, for we know that this cross – the pope's cross – is part of the mystery of the world's salvation which has been accomplished in Jesus Christ." Had this cross proved too heavy for one man to bear? Certainly John Paul I's early death was a warning against choosing someone whose health was fragile. The 111 conclavists looked closely at his abbreviated pontificate to see what could be learned from it. John Paul I had been elected for his pastoral qualities, for his ability to communicate with people, and in this respect their choice would appear to have been emphatically vindicated. During the *Novemdiales* sermons which preceded the conclave, Cardinal Confalinieri also pointed out that John Paul I had stressed "the integrity of faith, the perfection of Christian life, and the discipline of the Church." It was a deep hunger for the nourishment of solid spirituality which, according to Confalinieri, had drawn the crowds to the pope. There were those also, however, who had seen the image of the genial figure who loved children, the poor and the third world as dangerous because it had not

John Paul II arriving in Rome after his visit to Mexico.

been tested. His death according to some had been timely because it had spared him the problems on Puebla, on women priests or inter-communion. The way seemed to be pointing towards a people's pope but towards a pope who was also strong-minded and firm in his doctrinal teaching. Furthermore it was suggested that Pope John Paul I's ignorance of world affairs had placed him at a disadvantage. He had, for example, warmly received General Videla, President of Argentina, unaware that this might offend Latin American Catholics who were at that very time preparing a Puebla meeting intended as an unpleasant surprise to the military dictatorships with their "doctrine of national security". The need for someone who was politically aware and competent was made all the more poignantly obvious by the fact that shortly before the conclave, rockets were dropping upon the Maronite Christians of the Lebanon, and in Italy itself the Red Brigades were active again. In this election experience of world affairs must count as an important consideration.

Most of the important work in a papal election occurs before the actual conclave, as the cardinals meet, discuss and get to know each other. In an atmosphere of tension, for each one knew that he, like everyone else, was subject to close scrutiny, the lessons to be learned from what had gone before were thrown open for discussion, and with them the names of the most likely *papabile* (those candidates having the necessary qualities for pope), among them Cardinal Lorscheider, the man for whom John Paul I had consistently voted in the August conclave; Cardinal Siri of Genoa, an archconservative ardently supported by the Italian Catholic Press; Cardinal Benelli, the favorite of less reactionary Italians, and Cardinal Hume, strongly supported in London by both the *Times* and the *Guardian*.

As, however, the cardinals, wearing red cassocks, white surplices and red birettas gathered on the 14th October in the Pauline Chapel, beneath Michelangelo's frescoes of the crucifixion of St. Peter and the conversion of St. Paul, nothing was certain. Most, if asked as they processed in reverse order of seniority through the Sala Ducale, beneath Bernini's cherubs into the Sistine Chapel itself, would have considered another Italian pope most likely, but a non-Italian was by no means excluded. Indeed, during the mass "for electing the pope" Cardinal Villot, expounding on the Gospel of St. John, had placed all such considerations in their proper perspective by applying the verse "You have not chosen me, I have chosen you" directly to the conclave. Human abilities must be taken into consideration, but ultimately the mandate of the college of cardinals came from God's choice and not "from the human qualities that we may or may not possess."

The system of the conclave was first established in 1271 with the election of Gregory X. Since then the rules have been repeatedly modified but one factor has remained all-important – that of secrecy. The very name derives from the Latin *cum clave* meaning "with key" and refers to the fact that the cardinals are not allowed contact with the outside world. When, on Saturday 14th October, the cardinals began entering the crucible of the conclave, 88 other persons such as kitchen and medical staff were already in there, having taken a vow of secrecy which bound them on pain of excommunication from revealing what occurred during the course of the conclave. The cardinals too, must first listen to a solemn reading of parts of the apostolic constitution, *Romano Pontifici Eligendo*, and in particular Nos. 55-61 on secrecy. Anyone discovered using or planting "technical instruments, of whatever kind, for the recording, reproduction or transmission of voices and images" (No. 61) would have been instantly ejected at this stage. Then each cardinal took the oath of secrecy on the Gospels: "Above all, we promise and swear to observe with the greatest fidelity and with all persons, including the conclavists, the secret concerning what takes place in the conclave or place of the election, directly or indirectly concerning the scrutinies; not to break this secret in any way, either during the conclave or after the election of the new Pontiff, unless we are given special faculty or explicit authorization from the same future Pontiff (No. 49)."

Only then could the conclavists repair to their rooms or "cells" – some to dark little offices tucked away in obscure corners, their telephones carefully disconnected, others to huge Renaissance reception rooms hung with ornate chandeliers. The doors of the Sistine Chapel were sealed. The conclave had begun.

In view of the vow of secrecy, it is impossible to tell exactly what occurred in the course of the voting which began soon after nine o'clock next morning when the cardinals processed into the Sistine Chapel, took their places at the twelve wooden tables set out in rows, and cast their votes on cards headed with the words *"eligo in summum pontificem"* (I choose as the supreme pontiff). There has been some suggestion that Cardinal Karol Wojtyla had some intimation of what was to come. Certainly it is true that in the August conclave which elected John Paul I, seven votes had been cast for him and, while this was not a significant number, it did indicate that his name was one which had been given some consideration. Cardinal Stefan Wyszinski, the Primate of Poland, had told a group of friends in Poland that he could not envisage his fellow cardinal as Primate but rather that he was destined for "greater things" and with disturbing insight the woman whom Karol regarded "almost as my grandmother", Mrs. Irena Szkocka, had predicted his

Hands reach eagerly to greet him in Gniezno.

A moment of reflection in New York.

Apparently endorsing the view that Cardinal Wojtyla's election was not, at least initially, a strong likelihood, when the conclavists cast their votes and approached the altar in the Sistine Chapel, for the first time giving their oath: "I call to witness Christ the Lord who will be my judge that my vote is given to the one whom before God I consider to be elected", they seemed to be looking in accordance with tradition for an Italian pope. Dedicated observers of Vatican activity have produced what may be considered a fairly reliable account of the progress of the voting and in the first ballot the main contenders were Cardinal Guiseppe Siri of Genoa. Giovanni Benelli of Florence and Cardinal Pericle Felici. In the second ballot many of the votes previously cast for Felici went to Benelli, but still he failed to achieve the necessary two thirds plus one majority, and so during the first day the abortive struggle to find an Italian pope went on. As the day progressed, however, an increasing number of votes for non-Italians, among them Karol Wojtyla, began to emerge and by the end of the day, as black smoke rose once more from the stove in the corner of the chapel and appeared via a somewhat undistinguished flue above St. Peter's Square, the Cardinals must have realized that they were now looking for a non-Italian pope.

On Monday morning, on the sixth ballot, the number of votes for Wojtyla increased noticeably and it is said that he was so visibly shaken at the prospect that Cardinal Wyszinski, fearing that his friend might refuse the Papacy, took him to one side and reminded him that it was his duty as a cardinal to accept. The last ballot (it is not certain whether it was the seventh or the eighth) was conclusive. Then, with apprehensive solemnity, Cardinal Wojtyla was asked whether he would accept the election. With tears in his eyes, he paused so long before replying that many feared he would refuse, and when he finally did speak it was to refer to the words of Pope Paul VI's "Constitution on the Election of a Pope":

"We ask him who is elected not to refuse the office to which he has been elected for fear of its weight, but to submit himself humbly to the Divine Will; for God who imposes the burden sustains him with his hand lest he be unequal to bearing it; in conferring the heavy task upon him, God also helps him to accomplish it and, in giving him the dignity he grants him also the strength, lest in his weakness he should fall beneath the weight of his office."

In his former diocese of Kraków, 'Wujek' is not forgotten.

election many years previously. On her personal copy of the prophetic poem by the poet and playwright, Juliusz Slowacki, beside the words:

"He has made ready the throne for a Slav Pope,
He will sweep out the churches and make them clean within,
God shall be revealed, clear as day, in the creative world,"

she had written unwaveringly "This Pope will be Karol." It is perhaps true to suggest, however, that it is one thing to recognize in a person the qualities which will one day qualify him for "greater things" and another to attribute to him the private certainty of a specific happening. Friends and journalists who were with Wojtyla at the time of and shortly after his receiving the news of John Paul I's death, have noted that he was greatly disturbed by it and that he became absent-minded and remote, and have interpreted his reaction in the light of his knowledge that he might be the next to take upon himself the mission of Peter. The question of Cardinal Wojtyla's personal conviction must remain open. What is certain, however, is that when a news photographer was taking photographs of the cardinals before the conclave, Wojtyla laughingly remarked "Why are you taking so many photographs of me? You certainly don't believe I might be the next pope." His last act before disappearing into cell No. 91, assigned to him during the conclave, characteristically equipped with a quarterly review of Marxist theory, was to ask his Polish hosts in Rome to book him on the first plane to Krakow, without waiting for the installation ceremony of the new pope.

In carefully compiled Latin came the reply: "Knowing the seriousness of these times, realizing the responsibility of this selection, placing my faith in God, for Christ, for the Virgin Mary, the Mother of God, respecting fully the Apostolic constitution of Paul VI . . . I accept."

There was another long pause and then: "Because of my reverence, love and devotion to John Paul and to Paul VI, who has been my inspiration and my strength, I shall take the name of John Paul."

The conclave applauded and the master of ceremonies, acting as notary with two assistant masters as witnesses, drew up a document, a legacy to history, concerning the acceptance of the 264th Pontiff and the name taken by him.

Outside in St. Peter's Square an excited crowd of Romans and tourists had been waiting expectantly since the first morning of the conclave. For two days a large and motley assembly of churchmen, television crews, nuns, reporters, children carrying helium-filled balloons, and pick-pockets had been curiously united by an all-absorbing preoccupation with smoke-signals issuing from an otherwise nondescript stove-pipe in a cornice of St. Peter's. The most dedicated smoke-watchers had even brought their camp-stoves in order to avoid leaving the celebrated chimney to satisfy the demands of their less dedicated palates. Seven times the huge crowd had bubbled with excitement as smoke began to appear from the chapel, some had even begun to shout triumphantly "Viva il Papa", but seven times the chemical pellet, now used instead of the traditional wet straw, gradually turned the smoke black, and the crowd resigned itself to waiting once again. Reassuringly, a voice on Vatican Radio reminded its listeners that the average length of twentieth century conclaves was three days and that the conclave of 1922 had lasted seven days. By the evening of the second day there were those who could not help recalling that one nineteenth century conclave had lasted more than 50 days – and so the tension mounted. Then, at 6.18 pm, the smoke began to rise again, this time unquestionably white. "E bianca!" the crowd whispered, then shouted, cheered and clapped. The world had a pope – but who on earth was he?

As more and more Romans rushed from all parts of the city to the already packed square, the lights came on in the Hall of Benediction, the tapestry was unrolled from the balcony and while Pope John Paul II changed into his new vestments, of which Gammarelli's, the Vatican tailors, had provided a number of different sizes, Cardinal Felici appeared, smiling, on the balcony. In Latin he proclaimed "I announce to you a great joy. We have a pope." Then came the name: "Carolum Cardinalem Wojtyla . . . who has taken the name of John Paul." The crowd was at once astonished and delighted; astonished because their newly elected pope was a stranger, delighted because the man whom they gradually identified as a Pole had taken the name of his much loved predecessor. The air resounded with cheers and expressions of amazement as the realization slowly dawned that in electing the first non-Italian pope for 450 years the conclave had moved as far away as possible from the conventional certainty of old Rome and turned its back on centuries of tradition.

When, within the hour, Pope John Paul II appeared on the balcony to bless the crowd, he was greeted with all the warmth that the Italians, as a nation, feel for Poland as a land which has known so much suffering, the more so because their very first encounter with the new pope was in itself a breach of tradition. Tradition demanded that he merely gave his blessing – urbi et orbi – in Latin but this stranger chose to speak to them first in almost flawless Italian:

"Dear brothers and sisters, we are all still saddened at the death of our beloved Pope John Paul I and so the cardinals have called for a new bishop of Rome. They called him from a far-distant country – far and yet always close because of our communion in faith and Christian traditions. I was afraid to accept that responsibility, yet I do so in a spirit of obedience to the Lord and total faithfulness to Mary, our most Holy Mother. I am speaking to you in your – no, our Italian language. If I make a mistake, please correct me. I would like to invite you to join me in professing our faith, our hope and our fidelity to Mary, the Mother of Christ and of the Church, and also to begin again on the road of history and of the Church. I begin with the help of God and the help of men."

'It is cold up there on the mountain.'

If there had been doubters among the Roman crowd, these few words delivered with obvious emotion and in a voice which suggested both humility and strength, went straight to their hearts. He had used "I" instead of the ceremonial "we", he had identified himself as their bishop and he had corrected the words "your language" to "our language". Again the cheers soared into the night sky. When, finally, Pope John Paul II gave the Latin benediction, waved and disappeared, those who lingered in the square below were preoccupied by all the possible effects of a Polish pope upon the world at large, but the atmosphere was one of jubilation and above all one of excitement. To the people of Rome the man from Poland had appeared as a vision of dedication, faith and strength. In Poland, to the people who had known and loved him for many years, the pathos of the papacy was perhaps more readily apparent. In the Catholic weekly newspaper *Tygodnik Powszechny.* Tadeusz Zychiewicz drew attention to the private tragedy of those moments when the clapping and cheering stops: "It is a heavy and terrifying burden they have placed on his shoulders. It is cold up there on the mountain. With all our hearts we wish him the strength to bear the cold, knowing as we do that he will not only be cold but alone. May God be always near him". Those who were with Cardinal Wojtyla shortly after his election will recall a picture of him seated beneath Michelangelo's "Last Judgement", his head in his hands, his body slumped – already alone.

When, on the 16th October, news of a new era in the history of the papacy was broadcast to the world, congratulations were plentiful and so, too, were speculations as to the thinking behind the cardinals' choice. President Jimmy Carter's message of congratulations pinpointed some of the reasons why many believed the Polish cardinal had been selected: "I add my congratulations and my sense of joy to that felt around the world at your selection as Pope. Twice in eight weeks, the College of Cardinals has had to choose a new leader for your church and a spiritual guide for the world – and twice they have given us choices which have filled the Church and the world with new hope. Like your predecessor, Your Holiness has shared the experience of working people, and understands the daily victories and defeats of human life. As a theologian, a pastor, and a worker, you also understand the most extreme tests that life presents. You know what it is to struggle for faith, for freedom, for life itself, and your insight into these modern dilemmas will enrich, and be enriched by the enduring traditions of your Church."

In his home town of Wadowice, the election of John Paul II is celebrated with a Mass.

Beyond this kind of reasoning, it was claimed that John Paul II had been elected because he was well-connected and well traveled. His active part in the Second Vatican Council and his membership of the Synod of Bishops had brought him into contact with the "International Church" and he had traveled extensively in Europe, Canada, the U.S.A. and Australia. He was known to be a man of intellect, a linguist who spoke Italian, English, Spanish, French and Russian, and doctrinally a supporter of Vatican II. Like his predecessor he had the ability to draw people to himself; unlike his predecessor he was physically strong and at 58 was the youngest pope to be elected since Pius IX. His life had been a continued witness to pastoral experience, and as a Pole, he was, of course, the ideal person to cope with the threatening problem of euro-communism. Doubtless all these considerations were valid, but doubtless too, there were others equally well qualified in each of these different respects. Could it be that those attempting to reason in this way were falling into the very trap against which, on 21st October, John Paul II himself warned journalists; that of plunging "boldly into a far-reaching analysis of the problems and motives of Church personalities at the risk of passing over the most important aspect, which, as you know, is not political but spiritual"? Could it be that beyond the intellectual theorizing and the political speculation, the true reason for his election lay in the simple and perhaps unfashionably unsophisticated fact

that the cardinals recognized in him a man of God, a man of love? Significantly it was only those who did not know the man who were truly surprized at his election.

At the time of his election there were many who knew little or nothing about the new pope apart from the fact that he was a Pole. Before the conclave, "The Inner Elite: Dossiers of Papal Candidates" had asserted with great authority: "A study of the processes that bring a man to the cardinalate show the extent to which each has been given a certain mind-set and imbued with a given system of values. A key element is isolation from the normal influences of human experiences at an early age and immersion in a homogenized ecclesiastical culture." Now, either with a view to verifying this kind of theory or with a view to predicting more accurately what was to come, the world received with absorbed interest whatever snippets of information could be gleaned about the life of this man "from a far-distant country" and the small town of Wadowice, where the boy Karol had grown up, assumed overnight an overwhelming importance.

In looking at the early lives of those who have risen to positions of prominence, there is always a danger of viewing otherwise insignificant details in the light of what was to follow, and of seeking to show that the outcome, now known, was inevitable from the very beginning. Bearing this in mind the life story of a pope is, nevertheless, of interest and it is worth seeking beyond the hand-written entries which record Wojtyla's life in the Parish Register at Wadowice: Born 18th May 1920; baptized 20th June 1920; ordained priest 1st November 1946; consecrated bishop 28th September 1958; made archbishop 30th December 1963; became a cardinal 9th May 1967 and finally – 16.x.78. *in Summum Pontificem electus, Joannes Paulus II.*

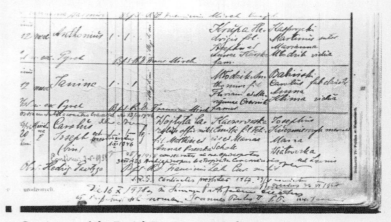

Section 71 of the Parish Register in Wadowice.

Karol Wojtyla was born in Wadowice, near Kraków, into a poor family. His father, after whom Karol was named, was a retired lieutenant of the Corps of Supplies, first in the Imperial Austro-Hungarian Army, then in the Polish Army, and his small pension permitted only a modest apartment on the first floor of number 7 Koscielna (Church) Street. Little is known of his very early years. His own writings are conspicuously lacking in autobiographical detail and it is possible that his parents were at this stage largely concerned with their elder son, Edward, who after proving himself to be of exceptional intelligence at his high school, had qualified as a doctor and was now hoping to become a consultant. It is known, however, that in 1927 Karol entered the "Universal" or primary school in Wadowice and that he remained there until he was eleven. A school photograph taken at this time shows him as a serious-faced boy with the close-cropped, almost scalped look of many of his Polish contemporaries.

Wojtyla was to have his first close encounter with tragedy early in life. In 1929, at the age of forty-five, his mother Emilia died and shortly afterwards the elder son, Edward, on whom so much hope had been focused, died tragically of an attack of scarlet fever contracted in the hospital where he was working. Inevitably these two deaths, occurring in rapid succession, left their mark on the boy. Monsignor Kazimierz Figliewicz, at Wawel

The house in Wadowice where Karol Wojtyla was born.

Cathedral in Kraków, who has known Karol from his earliest days, recounts how "looking closely at him, one could find traces of the experience". As a result Karol drew closer to his father, who was a loving but stern parent, and a believer in military discipline. Karol, or rather Lolek, as he was known to his friends, (Lolek is a frequently used diminutive of Karol) was subjected to a rigorous daily routine of mass, school, a meal, one hour's play, then homework followed by early bed. Discipline and hard work at an early age was to bring its rewards, however. In 1931 Karol and his friends moved to the boys' *Gymnasium* and there he earned the reputation of being something of a genius. He is remembered by teachers and schoolmates alike as being good at everything and yet, possibly even more remarkably, as being not a priggish but rather, a friendly and stimulating companion. Although while he was still very young he developed a life-long love of Polish literature, he was not totally absorbed in bookwork. His strong, stocky body was ideally built for any number of sporting activities: football, swimming, hiking, canoeing, and above all skiing in the Tatra mountains, which then as now formed a fundamental part of the psychic make-up of Wojtyla. Throughout his life the

With his father in Wadowice in 1928.

Tatras have been a place for meditation and a place of refuge in times of stress, but from his very earliest years they epitomized his love of freedom. It was at school too, that Wojtyla first showed his talent for dancing (he excelled at the complicated Polish folk dances) and for acting. He was an active member of the school drama group, so much so that he was entrusted with the time-consuming and challenging task of producing many of the plays himself.

From the accounts of those who knew Wojtyla as a child, he emerges as the almost too perfect all-round pupil, and working on the principle that there is no virtue in excellence if it comes too effortlessly, it is perhaps reassuring to note that piety is not the foremost quality for which he is remembered. Doubtless, however, Karol's

Karol with his mother, Emilia Wojtyla.

father's deep religious convictions left an impression on the boy and it must be noted that he served as an altar-boy each morning at mass. The parish priest whom he assisted harbored a secret hope, for some years, that Karol would one day choose the priesthood. It was a hope too, which was reiterated by the erstwhile Archbishop Metropolitan of Kraków, Prince Sapieha, who visited the school in Wadowice shortly before Karol was to take his school-leaving examinations. The boy with the sonorous voice and careful speech was chosen to welcome their distinguished visitor and he did so with such fluency and obvious ability that the Archbishop is said to have inquired whether Karol had shown any inclination towards the priesthood. A schoolfriend of Wojtyla's, looking back on their shared schooldays, remembers him as "somehow different". "He was remarkable for his versatility. He was in many ways an extrovert but what really set him apart from the rest of us was the other side of him, which could be reflective, contemplative, even mysterious." This delicate balance between extrovert and introvert and his wide range of talents led many to believe that Karol Wojtyla was destined for something special. When, however, at the age of eighteen he left school, having graduated top of his class, it was not with the intention of following the example of most Poles who excelled intellectually, and entering the priesthood, but with a view to joining the world of the theater.

In the same year, 1938, Karol and his father moved to Kraków, a city of magnificent art and architecture, dominated by the fortified castle on Wawel Hill, the home of a succession of Polish Kings and a proud historical seat, and by the adjacent Cathedral, one of Poland's greatest religious centers. An inscription on an effigy in the city describes Kraków in glowing terms: *Cracovia totius Poloniae urbs celeberrima* – "Kraków, most celebrated of all Polish cities" – but the eulogy was well founded, and remains so today, for not only did the golden age, when the city was the capital of the Jagiellonian dynasty linking Poland to Lithuania, leave a rich heritage of artistic masterpieces, it also gave to the world a great seat of learning, in the form of the Jagiellonian University.

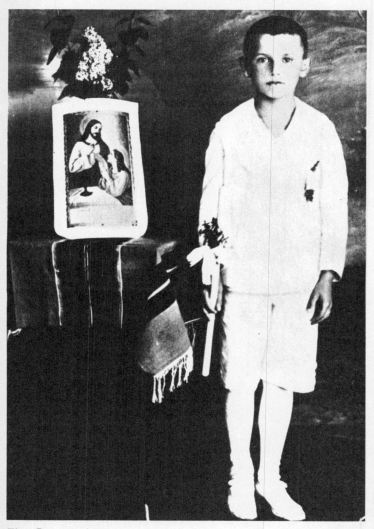

First Communion.

It was here that, after spending the greater part of his summer vacation working on the roads, Karol enrolled at the start of the new academic year. He joined the Department of Philosophy, one which already boasted an impressive number of scholars of international repute, to read for a degree in Polish language, literature and philosophy. Once again, his contemporaries at University remember him as a student of great academic ability but also as a young man who was good-humored, friendly and understandably popular. The subject he had chosen to study gave him an excellent excuse for joining the students' experimental drama group 'Studio Dramatyczne

1939', a theater workshop which experimented in developing new dramatic ideals. Here his hopes of becoming an actor seemed nearer fulfillment when he took part in the "Knight of the Moon", a drama based on an old Kraków legend. With his large, muscular frame and his beautiful, haunting voice, he played the part of Taurus, the bull, so convincingly that his fellow-players were determined he was destined for theatrical stardom. Wojtyla enrolled in optional elocution classes; in his spare time he began to study for a diploma in drama; he became one of the few privileged undergraduates permitted to join the élitist Polish Language Society and, in addition to all this, he still found time to write poetry and folkloristic ballads, after the style of the then popular Zegladowicz, which he recited during poetry-reading evenings organized by the students. By the end of his first year at University Wojtyla was deeply immersed in the academic life and almost oblivious to the distant rumblings of Nazi boots on the march across Europe, but this was all to change suddenly.

On 22nd August 1939, to the astonishment of the world, Germany and Russia signed a peace treaty. Allied to Russia, Germany's visions of walking over Europe seemed relatively unimpeded and when, on 1st September, Karol Wojtyla made his way to mass at Wawel Cathedral (for despite all his other activities, he had by no means abandoned the church), it was to the sound of bombs falling over Kraków. The Blitzkrieg offensive against Poland had begun. Within a few days the 14th Army had reached Kraków and the policy of exterminating Jewish and Polish *Untermenschen* began. A select few were to be preserved as servants and laborers for the Reich but intelligence and education levels were for obvious reasons to be kept to a minimum. The closing of the Jagiellonian University marked the beginning of an attempt to eliminate systematically the intelligentsia, the nobility and the clergy. Many of Kraków's academic staff were sent to Sachsenhausen concentration camp; some were subsequently released but most were never seen again.

Those academics who were not arrested did not, however, remain idle. Instead, they went underground, organizing themselves into groups, so that tutorials, seminars and examinations could be held secretly in private houses. Students were also in grave danger – to be identified as such meant death or removal to a concentration camp – but with grim determination that learning should not be denied by military oppression,

Karol Wojtyla senior (the man with the shaved head and moustache) in a school photograph. His son sits one place removed from him.

many continued to study at the "underground university". Among these was Wojtyla, who enrolled without hesitation as a second year student of philology. The way to avoid deportation was to show oneself to be useful as a laborer for the Reich. The possession of an *Arbeitskarte* (work card) meant some security at a time when those without one were instantly deported to the camps, and so Karol mingled with the working people and went to break stones with a sledgehammer in a quarry belonging to the Solway Chemical Works outside Kraków. Karol was later to be "promoted" to assisting the shot-firer by packing explosives into holes in the rockface and stringing up fuses and eventually he was transferred to the water purification department of the Solway factory, where he carried lime in buckets suspended from a wooden yoke. It was all hard labor, however, alleviated only by the company of friends. Among these were Juliusz Kydrinski, who had been in the same seminar group as Wojtyla at the Jagiellonian University and who was later to become a well-known writer, Krauze the quarry foreman, and the daughter of one of the factory directors who used to bring Wojtyla welcome snacks to restore his strength. Karol, despite the bitter cold and what amounted almost to convict labor, managed to find time for the humblest of the workers, trying to improve working conditions and helping to provide for their recreational, cultural and spiritual needs. The discipline of his childhood stood him in good stead. Karol studied at night, was one of the first to join the new underground Rhapsodic Theater as an actor and co-producer and still found time to write. Under the pseudonym of Andrzej Jawien he wrote articles later published in the Catholic newspaper *Tygodnik Powszechny*, plays on Biblical themes and poetry – poems which, like "The Quarry", speak with imagery that is both beautiful and powerful of work, of the workers, and of human emotions and which, despite the censors, point beyond the suffering to a God, who means salvation.

> "How splendid these men, no airs, no graces;
> I know you, look into your hearts,
> no pretence stands between us.
> Some hands are for toil, some for the cross . . .
>
> . . . Whoever enters Him keeps his own self
> He who does not
> has no full part in the business of this world
> despite all appearances."
>
> from "The Quarry" translated
> by Jerzy Peterkiewicz.

At this time Wojtyla was also profoundly influenced by a simple, uneducated ascetic with the very highest spiritual standards. Jan Tyranowski was a tailor by profession and also a dedicated Christian, with enormous spiritual strength, much of which was drawn from the writings of St. John of the Cross. It was he who introduced Wojtyla to the teachings of this sixteenth century mystic concerning the *via negativa*, and the concept of finding God in a darkness devoid of sensual pleasure may well have held a particular appeal at a time when such pleasures were few and far between. It was he who also organized the "Living Rosary" prayer circle of which Karol became a diligent member and he who formed the Catholic Youth Association of which the young student was at one time chairman. Despite the rigors of Nazi-occupied Poland then, Karol still managed to pursue his intellectual – and now, increasingly – his spiritual interests. The rigors, however, were not to be underestimated. Returning from work one night, Wojtyla collapsed with exhaustion in the street, only to be hit as he fell by a passing German truck.

Karol aged twelve.

Karol lay in the road, unconscious, with a fractured skull, until he was found next morning by a stranger who took him to hospital.

The precise point at which Karol Wojtyla abandoned his hopes of fame under theater spotlights and committed himself to a study of theology with a view to becoming a priest remains something of an enigma – so too do the

With his godmother, Maria Wiadrowska during the late thirties.

13

exact reasons for this apparently sudden change of course. The ever-imminent possibility of arrest and interrogation prevented the ready exchange of such confidences – even between the closest of friends – and even Karol's fellow-students at the illicit university remain uncertain at what stage the change in studies took place, although many have attempted to hazard guesses. Some have suggested that it was Karol's road accident which called him to revise his intentions and others claimed that a second, similar, accident only a short time later endorsed the call which he then decided to answer. Kydrinski recalls that in the early spring of 1941 Karol's father died while staying at the young writer's house. Wojtyla spent the entire night kneeling beside the body of the man who had been his pillar of strength and his point of reference on so many issues. At twenty Karol Wojtyla

The young Bishop of Kraków.

was left virtually alone in an exceptionally arduous world and this moment of extreme personal tragedy has been seen as the turning point in his life. No doubt these incidents had their role to play, but to see Wojtyla's decision as a "turning point" suggests perhaps too dramatic a change, for under the influence of his father, and later of Tyranowski, Karol had always been a committed Catholic. It is significant also that Karol himself did not recognize the gap between his dramatic and literary interests and his priestly vocation as so yawning a gulf. Later, as a well established priest, he was to write of the relationship between talent and vocation, "Priesthood is a sacrament and vocation, while writing poetry is the function of talent, but it is talent also which determines vocation." Also significant is the fact that beyond the romanticized image of a young man determinedly holding his own and helping others in defiance of enemy occupying forces, lay the brutal reality of suffering and

deprivation – his own and that of everyone around him. During the Nazi occupation Karol Wojtyla helped Jews to evade arrest by supplying them with Aryan identification papers, but for every one that escaped, countless others died from starvation, cold, punishingly hard work, bullets and ultimately from Cyclon B gas. Suffering either dispels or strengthens faith and the savagery of these years seems to have called Wojtyla to the service of others, for some time in 1942 Karol enrolled at the illegal theological department of the Jagiellonian University in the certain knowledge that discovery meant death.

While continuing his work at the Solway plant during the day, Karol studied at the underground seminary for two years. Then, in August 1944, shortly after the Warsaw uprising, Gestapo and SS Units purged the streets of Kraków in an attempt to discourage its citizens from attempting a similar insurrection. All males between fifteen and fifty found in the streets were rounded up, and shots were heard throughout the city, but Wojtyla, who remained quietly at prayer in the house which he shared with the Kotlarczyk family in Tyniecka Street, was not discovered. Nevertheless, Adam Sapieha, the same Archbishop Metropolitan of Kraków who some years previously had recognized the potential of the schoolboy welcoming him in Wodowice, took "Black Sunday" as a signal to gather his small, scattered group of seminarists into the archbishop's palace. Here, the imposing drawing room was equipped with twenty or so camp beds and converted into a dormitory for the seminarists, who were at last able to abandon their working clothes for black cassocks. They were to remain in the palace and study in the relative safety of the archbishop's protection. Archbishop Sapieha, although he stood for two of the things most ardently condemned by the Germans (he was both a prince of the church and a prince by birth), had remained conspicuously unafraid of them. When, occasionally, the German Governor General, Hans Frank, chose to afford him the dubious privilege of a visit, the old man took a defiant delight in serving him the coarse black bread and the beetroot conserve which formed the staple diet of the half-starved Polish people. For reasons best known to them, the occupiers had chosen to delay the elimination of this churchman, so beloved by the people of Kraków, and few dared to enter his precincts. Yet the dangers for Wojtyla were not altogether over. He continued to help distribute anti-Nazi newspapers and to assist Jewish families, and so found himself on a list of "unwanted persons". He was forced to abandon his work at the Solway Plant and the fact was of necessity reported to the German "Arbeitsamt". On the intervention of Adam Sapieha, however, Wojtyla's name was miraculously "lost" from the absentee returns submitted to the Germans, and for the remainder of the war the clandestine seminarist "disappeared" altogether from German eyes.

The war ended in Poland early in 1945, but the Russian "liberators" brought a very dubious "peace". In January a Government of National Unity was set up, with Wladyslaw Gomulka – one of the leaders in the A.L. Russian-backed Resistance Group – as Vice-Premier and Secretary-General of the Workers' Party, and the Moscovian Boleslaw Bierut as President of the Republic. Understandably, the exiled former Polish Government, now based in London, refused to acknowledge the new administration and so the bitter struggle, this time frequently of Pole against Pole, began again. It was in an atmosphere of tension and chaos that Wojtyla completed his studies to be a priest. He enrolled as a third year student at the reopened Jagiellonian University only narrowly to escape arrest once again, this time by the Russians, and it would merely have been for singing patriotic songs with a group of other young people in a church square, in a defiant and traditional cry for freedom. Fortunately, the group succeeded in dispersing in time and Wojtyla completed his studies. His overall performance was described by his professor, F. Rozycki as *emminente* i.e. more than excellent, and on 1st November, 1946, Karol Jozef Wojtyla was ordained priest by Archbishop Adam Sapieha, in the archbishop's private chapel. He celebrated his first Mass on the following day, All Soul's Day, in the crypt of St. Leonard in Wawel Cathedral.

ᙁ ᙁ ᙁ ᙁ ᙁ

Despite his unquestionably unconventional preparation for ordination, the talents of the new Father Wojtyla had not gone unnoticed. Once again Archbishop Sapieha intervened and Wojtyla was sent from a Poland struggling to recover from the westward shift of its frontiers (the Poles had regained, after 600 years, some of the half-obliterated cities of Germany and at the same time lost huge areas of land to the Russians), to the majesty and splendor of Rome. On a hill overlooking the city, the young priest spent two years studying at the Pontifical University Angelicum under the guidance of the Dominican Fathers. Here he wrote his dissertation on "The Concept of Faith in the Writings of St. John of the Cross". Significantly, the mystical poet, for whom faith appears as a series of paradoxes, had not lost his appeal with the end of the Occupation and, indeed, many years later, when Pope Paul VI called upon Cardinal Wojtyla to lead a Vatican retreat, he was still to draw on St. John's beautiful testimony to the paradoxes of a transcendant God:

> *"To attain to this which you know not*
> *you must pass through that which you know not.*
> *To attain to this which you possess not*
> *you must pass through that which you possess not*
> *To attain to this which you are not*
> *you must pass through that which you are not."*

The University dissertation, completed under the direction of a French Dominican who saw in St. John of the Cross a confirmation of the theses of Thomas Aquinas, was awarded nine points out of ten by the examining professors. The defence of the thesis was awarded fifty marks out of a possible fifty. Wojtyla's first venture outside Poland had won him academic acclaim and had placed him for the first time on the broad stage of the Universal Church. It had also given him a good command of Italian and his summer vacations spent among Polish exiles in the Pas de Calais and in Belgium had improved his working knowledge of French.

When, therefore, Father Wojtyla, D.D., left the cultural and intellectual sophistication of Rome to return to the Poland of 1948, it must have come as a surprise to many that he was sent as priest to a small parish apparently at the very end of the world. At that time Stalinist terror was at its highest pitch. In Poland the Communist Party was condemning even its own more moderate leaders – those who, although confirmed Communists, were looking for a Polish rather than a Soviet orientated communism. Secret police weeded out innocent people whose opinions were considered in any way "hostile", and prisons overflowed with the victims of unlawful and illicit arrests. While, however, in many parts of the country, people trembled at the sound of an early morning knock at the door, Karol Wojtyla presided over an old church in Niegowić surrounded by huge lime-trees, and a house set in a

kitchen-garden and orchard where chickens picked their way, undisturbed, through the vegetables. Perhaps the decision of Sapieha, now a cardinal, had not been so lacking in foresight. Certainly the villagers responded with warm appreciation to the man who arrived in Niegowić with only one small suitcase and placed himself entirely at their disposal. When one of his parishioners fell ill, the young priest would cheerfully take his place among the laborers in the fields, and pastoral visits to distant farms were undertaken on foot or on the back of a passing wooden cart. Tales of the kindness and generosity of Father Wojtyla are still told regularly in Niegowić today. In return, while Wojtyla was their incumbent, the villagers flocked to church and listened, enthralled, to the sermons of a priest whom they recognized to be "a truly good man".

When, after only one year, Wojtyla was transferred from Niegowić, he left behind him a brand new church, which he had helped to build, and a congregation of friends that he would retain for the rest of his life. Much to the amazement and confusion of his new parishioners in the busy parish of St. Florian's, in Kraków, the new priest arrived not in a taxi, but in the very least salubrious of farm carts, his worldly possessions were all mysteriously contained in a single suitcase and his faded cassock was punctuated with dark gray patches. The people of St. Florian's, at first dismayed by Wojtyla's lack of concern for

Wojtyla's first parish at Niegowić.

considerations of dress and physical well-being, were soon to discover that theirs was a priest who not only preached asceticism as a means of spiritual growth, but one who practiced it also. It is not known whether the man who is now Pope, like Pope John XXIII, swore a vow of poverty. What is known is that he frequently opted to sleep on the bare floorboards in preference to a comfortable bed; that at times he did not allow himself the luxury of sleep at all, passing the night in silent devotion in the church, and that all attempts to induce him to protect himself from the bitter Polish winter with overcoats, or even a cardigan, proved abortive. The congregation of St. Florian's grew to accept and admire his "unusual" ways and many recall with affection that at times the demand for him was so great that Wojtyla resorted to "hiding" in the confessional to snatch a few much needed moments for prayer and meditation. In particular he had an affinity with the young. Surrounding himself with students and young workers, he would organize cycle rides and hikes for them, accompany them skiing or simply take them into the mountains to speak to them of a God whom the Marxist educational system had attempted to oust altogether. They, in their turn, regarded him as an uncle, calling him *"Wujek"* (little uncle) and teasing him with friendly familiarity when, for example, he "switched off" i.e. lapsed into thought and ran off the road with his bicycle. He was also, however, the man to whom they turned for advice and whom they respected greatly, joining with him to say a "field" mass by the roadside, in a tent or in some laborer's cottage.

Work of this kind by a Catholic required much courage under Stalinism, but Karol Wojtyla gave himself up to it wholeheartedly. That is not to say, however, that he had altogether abandoned his love of the theater. There are still those in the offices of the Catholic monthly newspaper, *Znak*, in Kraków, who remember a shabbily dressed young priest clutching the notes for a play he was completing, on the subject of the Polish painter Brother Albert. Again the subject matter is interesting, for Brother Albert sacrificed his dedication to art to give his life to the poor. Wojtyla's identification with him is easily understandable. Yet by some strange ironic twist, or through the workings of some Divine Will, Wojtyla was compensated for the sacrifice of his dramatic career. The man who had surrendered the spotlights and the stage found himself addressing huge "audiences" every time he preached a sermon, for people came from miles around to hear his voice proclaiming the Gospel message, with obvious heartfelt sincerity and in a manner that was comprehensible to everyone.

Sadly for the people of St. Florian's, in 1951 Father Wojtyla's sermons were interrupted, for at the insistence of his former professor of theology at the Jagiellonian University, Fr Rozycki, Wojtyla decided to continue his academic studies. A few months previously, to the bitter grief of the people of Kraków, Cardinal Sapieha, their "invincible Cardinal" had died, and his successor, Archbishop Eugeniusz Baziak, granted Wojtyla dispensation from pastoral duties with a sabbatical for further studies. Wojtyla chose to pursue his interest in phenomenology and above all in Max Scheler, attempting to reconcile such contemporary theories with the traditional teachings of St. Thomas Aquinas. Scheler built largely on the "logic of the heart". Feeling is central to his work and love is the way by which goodness and other values are discerned. "Unless we love, we cannot know" is a premise fundamental to Scheler's teaching. It is a premise which has also exerted a lasting influence on Karol Wojtyla, and his thesis, entitled "The Possibilities for Building a System of Christian Ethics on the Basis of Max Scheler", in many ways foreshadowed all his later philosophy and his writings.

Wojtyla's work was accepted by the examining professor as a suitable dissertation for a junior professorship. It was presented in 1953 and approved in 1954, shortly before the Theology Department was closed down by the Communist authorities. However, once his teaching certificate had been obtained, Wojtyla was invited to give several lectures at the University of Lublin; the lectures gradually became a regular feature and after only two years he was offered the chair of Ethics. At thirty-six Wojtyla thus became a fully-fledged professor, the Head of Lublin's Institute of Ethics. Then, on 4th July 1958, the Pope appointed Professor Father Karol Wojtyla as titular bishop of Ombi and bishop auxiliary of the Kraków diocese. Wojtyla, Cardinal Wyszinski remembers, was out canoeing at the time. It was only after many hours

of trying that Poland's Primate managed to contact him, tell him of the Holy Father's wishes and ask him whether he accepted the appointment. "Yes", came the characteristic reply "but now can I go back to canoeing?" Within a matter of hours he was back on the lakes.

Wojtyla in the diocese of Kraków.

The consecration ceremony took place in Wawel Castle Cathedral on 28th September 1958. The day was damp and overcast and inside the cathedral the darkness was lightened only by spattering candles, but a story which has already become something of a legend tells, with all the poetic symbolism of a master painting how, as Wojtyla in accordance with the order of service raised his miter to the heavens, a shaft of warm sunlight penetrated the stained-glass windows and fell on the solitary figure of the newly-anointed bishop. The congregation of relatives, friends, parishioners from Niegowić and St. Florian's and even fellow workers from the Solway plant were convinced that here was one of the Lord's chosen.

WU WU WU WU WU

The new bishop himself obstinately refused to alter his life style to that of a man "set apart or above". As he was later to reaffirm in his retreat on the "Sign of Contradiction", he saw the kingly mission of Jesus Christ as handed on to the Church in a very special way in the pastoral authority exercised by the bishops under the direction of the successor to Peter, and by priests and deacons under the direction of their bishops, but this did not absolve them from respecting the "kingliness" in every man, which stems from Christ the good shepherd. "The bishop who visits the communities of his Church is the authentic pilgrim who arrives at one after another of the good shepherd's sanctuaries preserved by the People of God, sharers in the kingly priesthood of Christ". It was no part of a bishop's role to become separated from the other sharers in this kingly priesthood. Bishop Wojtyla still had the capacity to fill a church, but he wanted also to reach beyond the believers to those who doubted or even denied the faith to which he was so totally committed. Each week he opened his apartment for a party of a different kind. Professional people, students and workers, no matter what their creed or status, were invited to share a glass of wine and an *"oplatek"* wafer – a wafer of unleavened bread – which the Poles traditionally share with each other on Christmas Eve as a symbol of friendship and harmony. This would lead to discussion and, frequently, also to a joyful rendering of Polish folk songs. These evenings were the beginning of other activities. Marxists, Roman Catholics, intellectuals, laborers – all would set off on outings organized by Poland's youngest bishop, who was still dressed in a threadbare cassock, still traveling through the streets on a bicycle, and still living in a tiny, two-room apartment.

It was while he was Bishop of Kraków that Wojtyla fell ill. The recommendation of his doctor was that to prevent any recurrence he should take plenty of exercise. The bishop needed no second bidding and the doctor's orders merely added more justification to what he was already doing, for in between his official commitments and his other pastoral duties, he was still cycling, kayaking and skiing with groups of enthusiastic students. With them he seemed to relive his own student days and sometimes indulged in most "unbishoplike" behaviour. One American lady in particular must have been very surprised to discover that one of the group who serenaded her, as she lay in hospital with a broken leg, was the Bishop of Kraków.

In 1962, on the death of Archbishop Baziak, Wojtyla was elected Vicar Capitular and so to all intents and purposes was placed in charge of the diocese. Then, on 30th December 1963, Paul VI appointed him Archbishop of Kraków, and on 18th January 1964 he took over as Archbishop Metropolitan. Still Wojtyla obstinately ignored the comments of the Metropolitan curia that his cramped lodgings were unsuitable for an Archbishop. The curia scored one of their few victories over him, however, while he was away from Kraków for a few days. In his absence they went to his lodgings, removed his few personal possessions and deposited them in the Archbishop's Palace. Wojtyla, on his return, was furious and when he did finally admit defeat and move to the Palace it was only to baffle the housekeeper by arriving bearing a canoe and paddles. She had never seen such unorthodox ecclesiastical accoutrements.

The Archbishop's Palace in Kraków is an imposing building with spacious rooms proudly displaying priceless paintings and furniture that once belonged to Polish Kings. Even here, however, Archbishop Wojtyla managed to secure himself a small, spartan bedroom more suited to his tastes. His frayed cassock was a constant source of embarrassment to his chauffeur and he was always penniless. He determinedly refused all payment for his professorship at the University of Lublin and what salary he did receive vanished without trace in the direction of those he considered to have greater need of it. Father Pieronek, who acted as Wojtyla's secretary when he traveled to Rome in 1967 to receive his cardinal's hat, recalls that on that occasion the cardinal had no red socks. The Felicjanki Sisters' Convent had presented him with the robes, but en route to the Sistine Chapel Wojtyla realized that his only socks were black. The Roman shops near the Chapel proved to be sadly lacking in red socks, so too did the cardinals' laundry at Santa Marta and so, even on this auspicuous occasion, Wojtyla's appearance was not what his chauffeur might have wished.

Karol Wojtyla's energy was apparently endless and every minute of his day was carefully planned. Starting at 5 a.m., the first hours of the day were generally allocated to a Mass, prayer, reading and above all to seeing people. His office was always open from 11 a.m. until 1 p.m. for anyone wishing to see him and he always made a point of visiting the poor and the sick – even in the early hours of the morning. When Kydrinski's mother lay dying in Kraków hospital, the Archbishop left his bed in the middle of the night to be with her during her last hours. Driving round the city, Karol would work in the back of the car on papers and books drawn from what seemed a bottomless briefcase. He also had the disconcerting ability to read or write while conducting a conversation and still recall exactly what was said. Many, too, will vouch for the fact that Wojtyla never forgets his friends, colleagues, parishioners or any of the multitude of people who have helped him in his life. At Christmas he went without fail to visit the workers at Solway whose loyalty he has never forgotten.

Yet, despite his heartfelt commitment to the duties of his office and to the people who surrounded him, Wojtyla managed to remain an avid sportsman throughout the twenty years in which he presided over Kraków. Asked once whether it was quite becoming for a cardinal to ski, Wojtyla replied unhesitatingly "It is not becoming for a cardinal to ski badly". This was not one of the Kraków cardinal's failings for it is not for nothing that he has been called the "Scourge of the Tatras". Dressed in baggy trousers and using old-fashioned skis – for he emphatically refused to spend money on new ski equipment – he would snatch a few hours in the mountains, often to the

Cardinal Wojtyla receiving his cardinal's hat from Pope Paul VI.

amazement of others whom he encountered on the snowy slopes. On one occasion in particular he is said to have lost his way, when skiing alone, and crossed the Czech border by accident. Discovered by a Czech patrol, he was arrested and held for some considerable time by security police who refused to believe that the man before them was really, as his official documents suggested, the Cardinal of Kraków.

☖ ☖ ☖ ☖ ☖

Tales of this kind concerning the man who now sits at the head of the gigantic apparatus of the Roman Catholic Church are endless. When a man is elected pope he runs a grave risk of disappearing behind a formal image and a cloud of somewhat informal mythology. In the nineteenth century Alphonse Daudet wrote a poignant story about a small boy who repeatedly stayed out late, playing. When he returned to confront the wrath of his parents, he would announce solemnly "le pape est mort" (the pope is dead). The effect was so devastating that when his family awoke in the morning and found that the pope was not dead, they were so pleased that they forgot to punish the boy. The story illustrates admirably simply, although naturally with some degree of poetic exaggeration, the legendary stature and importance which the life, or indeed the death, of one man assumes overnight, when he becomes the successor to Peter. The formality which traditionally surrounds the papacy, the style of dress and the style of address, are all designed to raise the pope from the level of the individual to the level of the universal and archetypal, from that of the human to that of something much greater than human. John Paul II had to shield the swimming pool at his summer residence at Castelgandolfo

before he could swim in it. "Naked he appears but a man" must surely have been the principle underlying the Vatican statement that some people would take offence at seeing the pope in a swimming costume. In view of this, it is understandable that there are those who seek to "humanize" their spiritual father. Less understandable is the fact that attempts to show that the pope is a man like any other have exactly the opposite effect. Strangely, the knowledge that Pope John Paul II has carted piles of frozen excrement from the blocked lavatories left by the SS in the Theological Seminary used as their headquarters during the Occupation, serves only to enhance and not to detract from his mystique.

Those who, in the days following the election of John Paul II and preceding his inauguration, scrutinized the life that had gone before, were concerned not so much with the "human element", as with the element that had placed him in a position where the demands were almost superhuman. Bearing in mind the requirements outlined in "The Inner Elite. Dossiers of Papal Candidates" they glanced briefly at his personal life, noted with some surprise that in some ways he had not been "isolated from the normal influences of human experience at an early age" and then turned to the "ecclesiastical culture", to his public life – to his role in the church both in and outside Poland. After all, the fact that a man is a good skier does not make him pope, nor does the fact that he is a poet and nor, the more cynical might argue, does the fact that he is sincerely committed to the service and the love of people. More significant, many suggested, was the fact that he was Polish, for to be Polish meant to come from a land where nationalism and Catholicism were irrevocably linked and where Catholicism had proved itself to be the effective enemy of oppression and the champion of

His Holiness among the Polish community in Rome.

human rights. It meant that Pope John Paul II had survived the paradox of a country in which the Polish Communist Party officially holds the monopoly of power over a population which is overwhelmingly Roman Catholic.

In the year AD 966 the Polish ruler, Miezko, married a Christian princess from Bohemia and in doing so, himself became a Christian, thereby bringing Poland under the jurisdiction of the Church of Rome. The adoption of Roman Catholicism removed the main pretext for the German encroachments which Poland repeatedly suffered, but it also turned "Polania semper fidelis" into an exposed limb of Catholicism on the eastern boundaries of Central Europe. Successfully combated attacks from both East and West increased its sense of national identity and on the strength of this Poland elected to identify itself with Rome. When Boleslaw, Miezko's son, persuaded the pope and the Holy Roman Emperor to make the diocese of Gniezno an archbishopric it not only gave Poland independence from German ecclesiastical hierarchy, but also strengthened the links with Rome. Polonia became a sovereign state in 1024 by virtue of the pope's permission and so began a long tradition in which the equation of Pole and Roman Catholic became the symbol of the separate identity of the nation, a symbol which has endured to the present day.

The Poland into which Wojtyla was born was a young nation which had risen like an independent phoenix from the fire of the First World War. He belonged to the first generation of free Poles for nearly one and a half centuries. Three months after his birth the Red Army was defeated at the gates of Warsaw and the new nation began courageously to rebuild its thousands of demolished buildings with renewed faith in the future and a faith in God and the Virgin Mary, which had been increased and strengthened by the oppression of the nineteenth century. Religion had indeed served as the "mainstay of the people" during the days of the Partitions, for the Russians, Prussians and Austrians had all ruled their respective parts of Poland with an iron hand. During Wojtyla's early youth, however, the prevailing atmosphere was one of triumphant hope. Then came the German Occupation. Once again, it was the Church which led the struggle against the Nazis. One thousand Polish churches were destroyed by enemy action during the Second World War and three thousand priests were killed or lost their lives in concentration camps. There were many among the clergy who showed exceptional bravery, but of these one man in particular must be remembered, not only because he epitomizes the Christian Spirit, but also because of the interpretation Wojtyla placed upon his death.

Father Maksymilian Kolbe was well known throughout Poland as the guiding light in one of the world's largest monasteries, Niepokalanów. Together with his friars he built here not only a center for prayer, but also a completely self-supporting community which included among its many facilities a printing press compiled of all the most modern equipment. From here, in 1935, he launched a daily Catholic newspaper which was soon to become one of Poland's best-selling publications. In September 1939, however, the Nazi forces took over this flourishing center and many of the religious community were deported to Germany. Among them was Father Kolbe. This particular imprisonment lasted only a short time. In December, Father Kolbe, wracked with tuberculosis and suffering painful abscesses, was released and instantly began a mission for Polish refugees. He also wrote articles in his magazines designed to prick the consciences of the Nazi persecutors. So it was that in 1941 the priest who had made such a courageous stand for

Pope John Paul II in the Vatican in March, 1979.

freedom, was arrested for the second time by the Germans and sent to become prisoner 16670 in Block 11 at Auschwitz. Subjected to constant blows, flagellation and starvation because he refused to deny his faith in Christ, Father Kolbe was eventually incarcerated in this, the camp prison known to the inmates of Auschwitz as the Block of Death. It was in Block 11 that the court sessions were held, passing up to a hundred death sentences in the hour, in the name of some satanic justice. Once sentenced, prisoners were made to undress. The lucky ones were then afforded the dignity of dying with their faces turned to the wall outside in the courtyard; the not so lucky were simply executed in the lavatories. Many never even reached the courtroom, but died in one of the block's infamous cellars, where they suffocated in the heat and the stench or simply starved to death. One thing was certain – no-one who entered Block 11 ever came out alive.

Father Kolbe, initially in Block 14, was brought to one of these cellars following the successful escape of a prisoner. The camp authorities demanded the death of ten men as a reprisal. The prisoners of Block 14 were paraded before an SS officer who selected at random ten men to die of starvation in a windowless underground bunker. Father Kolbe was not among the chosen victims, but as one of the prisoners cried out in despair, a figure stepped out of the ranks and offered to take his place. "Who are you?" asked "Butcher" Fritsch, amazed. "I am a Catholic priest" came the reply.

In the wretched, stifling atmosphere of an underground cell in Auschwitz, Father Kolbe led his companions in fervent prayer, and hymns resounded through the concrete corridors. As one by one the starving wretches collapsed and died, Father Kolbe continued to comfort, to reassure and above all to pray. Finally, after a fortnight, only the priest and three other prisoners remained. The authorities, needing the cell, decided that their victims were taking too long to die, and sent a common criminal to accelerate the process. Father Kolbe, his face still calm and radiant, himself gave his arm to the executioner to receive an injection of phenol.

On 17th October 1971, Maksymilian Kolbe was beatified by Pope Paul VI and at Auschwitz in 1972, on the first anniversary of the beatification, Cardinal Wojtyla addressed a multi-national audience: "Auschwitz" he said "is a place in which the command to love was replaced by the imperative of hatred" . . . "But God's Providence manifested itself at last, towards the end of that terrible time of trial of which Auschwitz has remained the ultimate symbol. The life and death of Maksymilian Kolbe show the power of love victorious over hatred, and of the power of the human spirit to survive."

To Wojtyla also, the most crucial factor in the story of the blessed Maksymilian Kolbe was his reply to the inquiry of the SS man, Fritsch – "I am a Catholic priest." Throughout Wojtyla's life the figure of Father Kolbe was to act as a model of what priesthood represented, for it was in his capacity as a Roman Catholic priest that Kolbe sacrificed his life to be a source of comfort and love in the last terrible hours of his fellow sufferers. Priesthood is an "expression of the meaning given to man and the world by their relationship with God" and the true priest "simply by being who he is, expresses this meaning and at the same time conveys it to the world and to man in the world." Oppression and persecution serve only to make this meaning, as expressed in the priesthood and in the Church, more apparent.

❦ ❦ ❦ ❦ ❦

At the time when Karol Wojtyla was ordained priest, shortly after the conclusion of the Nazi occupation, the Provisional Government was treading carefully in its relations with the Roman Catholic Church. It regarded Catholicism as an irrelevant vestige of a bygone era and fully intended to oust the Church completely in the course of time but, for the moment, its primary interest was in the consolidation of its own power. Indeed, overt confrontation with so influential a force as the Roman Catholic Church in Poland would be, at least, embarrassing. Ironically, both Hitler and Stalin contributed to giving the Church the strong position it now occupies in Poland. Hitler's systematic slaughter of Polish Jews, and Stalin's annexation of the eastern provinces with their large Greek Orthodox and Uniate population, raised the proportion of Roman Catholics among the Polish population to more than ninety percent. This fact, coupled with the Church's greater strength as a spiritual, historical and patriotic force, called for caution on the part of the Communist Government, and Poland became the point of measured confrontation, co-existence and dialogue between Marxism and Catholicism. This does not mean to imply, however, that there were no acts of open hostility between the two bodies. As early as 1945 the government suspended the Concordat with the Vatican, for example. At Yalta the agreement between Churchill, Roosevelt and Stalin had endorsed Russia's claim on Poland's eastern territories, and the Potsdam agreement had attempted to compensate for this loss by restoring to Poland the ancient Slav territories which for 600 years had been under German rule. The shifting of Poland's frontiers naturally made her the target for German resentment and the Vatican refused to appoint diocesan bishops to the new Polish territories, or even to recognize the post-war frontier until a peace treaty was concluded.

No doubt the Soviet-orientated government would have revoked the Concordat in any case, but the attitude adopted by the answering anti-Communist Pope, Pius XII, provided a pretext for the government to "defend Polish National interests". In 1948 a number of Church organizations, among them Catholic Action, were officially declared illegal. Two years later, Cardinal Sapieha and Stefan Wyszinski, the newly appointed Archbishop of

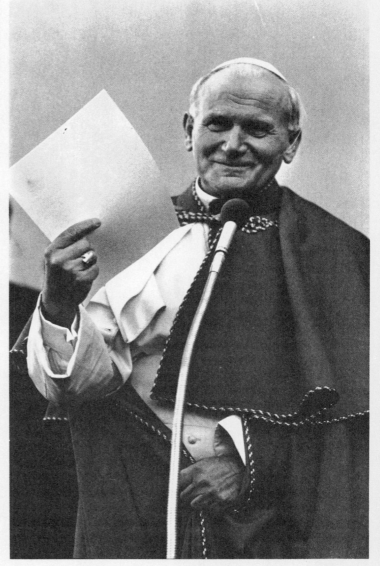

John Paul II at Mentarella in October, 1978.

Warsaw, complained to President Bierut, who was also First Secretary of the Party, that the Government was acting in bad faith in its dealings with the Church and the government reciprocated by accusing the bishops of adopting an attitude of hostility towards the People's Republic. On 14th April 1950, Communist representatives signed a paper recognizing the Pope as supreme head of the Church in all matters relating to church order and to faith, and in exchange the bishops acknowledged the restored western territories as part of Poland and agreed to appeal to Pius XII to appoint bishops for the new Polish dioceses. Accordingly, Cardinal Sapieha went to Rome and begged the Pope, on bended knee, to accept the compromise. Pius XII remained intractable, however, and in Poland, mistrust of the Vatican's *Ostpolitik* increased.

The relations between Church and government grew progressively worse under Stalin's regime. In the Autumn of 1953, Wyszinski, now a Cardinal, was confined to a monastery, where he was to remain interned for three years, and by the end of the year eight bishops and nearly one thousand priests had been arrested. The number of arrests increased rapidly in the following year and depression prevailed throughout Poland until the death of Stalin, and Kruschev's denunciation of his crimes. Then hope was born again, for when in 1956 Gomulka came to power it was to promise to follow "the Polish road to socialism". In an expansive gesture of good will, he released all those who had been imprisoned for their faith and re-instated Cardinal Wyszinski as Primate. The persecutions were not, however, over; the struggle had merely become more subtle. It was a battle between ideologies for the souls of the nation's young, for their commitment either to Poland, the model home of the "new man", or to Poland, the historical bastion of Christianity. As a young priest, Wojtyla would not, it may be argued, have been involved with the fluctuations of the highly complex relationship between Church and State, yet the most tragic aspect of the struggle lay in the fact that it sought to strike at the heart of Everyman and that it intruded, unwelcome as it was, into everyday lives. Perhaps nowhere is this fact more poignantly expressed than in the first socialist new town of Nowa Huta, where the church of the Mother of God, Queen of Poland, now rises proudly and eloquently from the junction of Karl Marx and Great Proletariat Avenues. The history of this soaring, concrete tribute to freedom and to faith provides an admirable example of how, in a city built "without God", the determination of its citizens prevailed, in defiance of persistent opposition from the government.

The town of Nowa Huta was built in the early 1950s around the massive Lenin Steelworks, not far from

The Pope returns to Rome after a visit to his homeland to be greeted by Giulio Andreotti.

Kraków. It was intended as a showpiece for socialism, the model home for the model socialist man who would not, of course, wish to live in the religious and reactionary atmosphere of historic Kraków. Disregarding all financial considerations, the government generously erected the

John Paul II with President Giscard d'Estaing of France.

concrete jungle they believed to be socialist man's heart's desire – wide roads imaginatively named, gray high-rise flats and a huge bronze statue of Lenin. Everything was provided except a church, a facility which, it was anticipated, the new man would not require. Unfortunately the new man, much to the embarrassment of the authorities, decided that the one item most essential to his needs was a building in which to worship God. Persistent attempts to dissuade him failed miserably and in 1957 permission to build a church was finally granted, and a site was allocated for the purpose. The people of Nowa Huta immediately had the site blessed, and a cross marked the spot where their new church was to be constructed. Then, in 1960, the government decided that instead of the promised church, they would build a school on the site and sent workmen to remove the wooden cross. The workmen met with hundreds of believers who defended the land, which they had already been using as a place of open-air worship, with a barrage of stones. Police replied with tear gas and severe penalties were meted out on the "rioters" but the cross remained and the faithful continued to assemble for regular Masses, held there despite the rigors of the climate.

Among those who celebrated mass on this unusual site was Karol Wojtyla. As bishop and archbishop, Wojtyla was constantly involved in arguments and discussions regarding Nowa Huta's church. Abhorring any incitement to violence, he nevertheless used every conceivable means of putting pressure on the authorities. Finally, in 1967, permission was given to build. A huge crowd gathered for a celebratory Mass in the open air, dampened by a persistent drizzle. Under their umbrellas the people knelt to pray in the mud beside a foundation stone which came from the tomb of St. Peter in Rome, and which bore a message from Pope Paul VI: "Take this stone to Poland, and may it be a corner-stone on which a church will stand at Nowa Huta dedicated to the Queen of Poland". The delays and obstructions were by no means over, however, and it was not until 1977 that the church stood in its entirety. On 15th May, it was finally consecrated by Cardinal Wojtyla. The apparently simple requirement to build a church had meant seventeen years of determined effort. It had involved argument and suffering, but the completed building, with its Chapel of Reconciliation containing the moving sculptures entitled "Christ in Auschwitz", is a living monument to the fact that in Nowa

Huta at least, as Cardinal Wojtyla proclaimed: "the will of God and the people who worked here prevailed". He added: "Let this be a lesson!".

The fight for the church in Nowa Huta was just one of numerous confrontations in which Wojtyla, as he rose in the ecclesiastical hierarchy, became increasingly involved. In 1966 Cardinal Wyszinski decided to celebrate one thousand years of Polish Christianity in a highly distinctive fashion. While exiled in a monastery he had read Sienkiewicz's account of the famous victory of the Poles over the Swedish invaders in 1655. According to Sienkiewicz, on the eve of this all important battle the ruler John Kasimir swore on oath on behalf of the nation to serve God and the Blessed Virgin, to rid Poland of foreign invaders, and to improve the social conditions of the Polish people. Wyszinski's idea was to call upon the people of Poland to make a similar but suitably adapted commitment during the years of preparation which culminated in the millennium celebrations. In 1956 the bishops led the country by taking a vow at Czestochowa, and so began a series of sermons and catechesis designed to make all Polish Catholics aware of their responsibilities.

Wojtyla as bishop, and subsequently archbishop, was deeply involved in these preparations and it is interesting to look more closely at the kind of promises Wyszinski, and with him Wojtyla, called upon the Polish people to make. In the course of the preparations they were asked to commit themselves to:

1) allegiance to God, the cross, the gospels, the church and her shepherds and to the sacred land of their fathers
2) fighting against their national vices
3) doing everything to help the nation's children to live in a desire for justice
4) defending the sanctity of marriage, and guarding the family unit, so that within that unit Poland's people can live peacefully and without fear
5) testifying to their devotion to the Mother of God and following her virtues
6) retaining in every Polish soul the grace which is the source of divine life
7) guarding, with eyes turned to the crib at Bethlehem, all unborn life
8) educating the young generation in loyalty to Christ
9) defending the sanctity of marriage and promoting Christ's rule in family life.

The list is, in its entirety, an act of outright defiance of the government. It is also characteristically Polish and characteristic of Wyszinski in its nationalism, traditionalism, tenacity in faith and its Mariology. More significant to those who wished to place Wojtyla in the context of a specific ecclesiastical culture is the stress on family life – the product, it may be suggested, of a society in which the family unit is one of the few areas which has remained to a large extent outside the reach of Communist indoctrination – and the determination to protect unborn life. In recent years, the government in Poland, thinking to win the loyalty of the people away from an unsympathetic church, has made abortion legal; the Church, scorning such cheap tactics, has remained unwavering in its attitude both to this and to contraception.

Examples of government harassment are numerous. In 1970 Gomulka was deposed after bloody riots in the Baltic coastal cities, and his replacement by Edward Gierek again brought a thaw in Church-State relations. By 1973, however, the Church and the State were once again at loggerheads, this time over the question of religious education. Official reports emphasized the need for a unified educational system designed to prepare young people for adult life in a "socialist" Poland. The school timetables were to be so arranged that it would be impossible for children to attend church for religious instruction. The bishops' response was vehement. "Such intentions", they argued, "could deny a person his fundamental right to freedom of conscience and religion which are guaranteed by the Polish constitution. State laws cannot be contrary to God's laws otherwise they are not binding." Riots in 1976 over steep rises in the price of food brought further friction. Wojtyla, together with other church leaders, announced publicly that the people had a right to protest. The Polish bishops took up the issue of religious freedom in a pastoral letter which pointed out that the State was using the people's taxes to propagate atheism in a country which was indisputably and overwhelmingly Roman Catholic. In a sermon at Nowa Huta, Cardinal Wojtyla underlined grievances which were very close to the hearts of the steelworkers: "The government does not allow you to be promoted because of your beliefs, nor are you allowed to worship in a building." Then on the Feast of the Epiphany he made one of his most memorable and characteristic addresses: "It is difficult from the point of view of human dignity, from a humanistic point of view, to accept atheism as a political program. For it is understandable that a man may seek but not find; it is understandable that a man may deny; but it is not understandable that a man may find himself forbidden to believe. If you wish to fill a given office, to reach a given position, you are forbidden to believe. Atheism as the foundation of national life is a painful misunderstanding from the point of view of true human progress. For it is necessary to respect what is in man."

He went on to stress the obligation of the faithful to speak out against the enforced imposition of an ideology which was contrary to the conviction of the majority. This was not the impassioned plea of a naive champion of religious faith, but rather the product of a deep rooted and carefully formulated humanism which recognized that freedom must apply to all, not only to Christians. "We do not wish to interfere with the families of atheists – that is a matter for themselves and their own consciences." This was the very essence of Wojtyla's approach to Communism.

Paradoxically, government harassment, intended to restrict the influence of the Church, in practice stimulated it and retarded the process of secularization which was taking place in other parts of Europe. Conflict acted as a stimulus to faith: this was the principle which lay at the roots of Wyszinski's attitude. Wojtyla on the other hand was frequently more conciliatory. When Pope Paul VI made Archbishop Wojtyla a cardinal, the event was seen by many as a political move, as an attempt to "counteract" the intransigent Wyszinski with the younger, suppler Wojtyla. Whatever the reasoning behind the actual appointment, the Polish government no doubt hoped to exploit the differences between the two men. The government failed miserably – the Cardinals remained united in their stand – but the difference in approach remained marked.

Wojtyla, like Wyszinski, would never compromise his principles, but he had the ability to place Church-State relations on the level of controlled dialogue. Wyszinski distrusted intellectuals, Wojtyla was able to meet them on their own terms. He has a breadth of culture and a profound understanding of Marxism which challenged the Marxists on their own ground, and frequently exposed their lack of knowledge of their own subject. The subtlety of his approach lay in his ability to score points without actually forcing the government into a position where violence was the only resort. He recognized the need to give Polish nationalism its voice without permitting it to shout too provocatively. Wojtyla, while avoiding, wherever possible, direct interference with temporal power, did not hesitate to speak out where necessary for human rights and human values – for liberty, respect for life, fairness, conscientiousness, the dignity of man and a spirit of reconciliation. It was values such as these which, according to him, formed the basis of a harmonious society. His dialogue with Marxism was more, it seemed, a dialogue with atheism, for he was not so much concerned with political Communism as with the challenge which atheism and agnosticism represented to the Christian way of life, and to those values contained in man which make him worthy of respect. Even here, however, Wojtyla had no illusions but talked on the basis of full reciprocity and exchanged concessions.

So, like Cardinal Wyszinski, Cardinal Wojtyla became within Poland a symbol of the Church's resilience, and indeed a symbol of all those trying to retain human dignity. His voice has frequently resounded as loudly as the Primate's on such issues as education – the re-opening of the Theological Faculty at the Jagiellonian University, access to the media, elimination of censorship, the building of churches, freedom from atheistic propaganda and the right to religious instruction. The list of protests is endless, but all came under the broad heading of "human rights", and all were undertaken with a distinctive combination of strength and flexibility which won him the respect of even the staunchest Communist leaders.

Because of its Communist government Polish society is of necessity restrictive, and there is no reason why a voice crying out for human rights within Poland should automatically make a resounding impact on the eardrums of the rest of the world. If Wojtyla came to the notice of the International Church as bishop, archbishop and cardinal it was possibly not so much because of his work within Poland but because of his attendance at, and contribution to, the Second Vatican Council, which brought him to the forefront of Church affairs and which also exposed him to churchmen whose experiences had been very different from his own.

The Pope prays at the spot where the body of Aldo Moro was discovered.

In Kraków, Wojtyla is known as a man upon whom the Council made an indelible impression, and whose ideas and teachings developed very much in its spirit. An examination of the Council, and of Wojtyla's role within it, might, therefore, be a good indication of what kind of papacy the world was about to witness.

On 2nd January 1959, Pope John XXIII announced to an astonished assembly of cardinals his intention of holding a council. His aim was to "spring-clean" the Church of Rome, for central to his belief had always been the idea that the Church, although it possessed the essence of eternal truth, must always be ready to re-interpret it in the light of the Gospel. Wojtyla, who was from the very first an enthusiastic supporter of this Council "inspired by the Spirit of Wisdom and of Love", saw as its starting point the awareness of a crisis situation; a situation arising from a growing indifference to ideology in a society orientated towards consumption and the worship of technology, and oblivious to altruistic values. Given this starting point, the Second Vatican Council was to concern itself with the entire human race, its values and the position of the Church within it. Significantly, Wojtyla considered that one of the prime objectives behind Pope John's summoning of the Council was that of Christian Unity. Asked while the Council was still in session what he anticipated the principal changes brought about by it would be, he replied that he believed that there would be a development of ecumenism on an unprecedented scale, accompanied by an upgrading of the role of the laity in the Church. There would also be an attempt to work out a new Church-State relationship and a new conception of the right to religious freedom. Catholicism would become more universalized, with a different approach to the ancient cultures of non-European people, i.e. de-westernized, and the Church itself would be decentralized by a revaluation of the bishop's authority and a return to the collegiate principle. Finally, he believed that pastoral methods would be reviewed and new ones introduced. In the light of what has already been seen of his life, the emphasis on religious freedom and tolerance and on pastoral care is almost to be expected. The stress on collegiality, which without impairing the primacy of the pope nevertheless distributes greater authority among the bishops, is of interest in view of what was to follow.

It was touch and go whether Wojtyla would be granted a visa to attend the opening session in 1962, but the authorities relented in time and Wojtyla, speaking to the assembly on liturgy and on the sources of revelation, impressed many of the foreign clerics, not least for his command of languages (the proceedings in the first session were conducted in Latin) and for his youthful enthusiasm. It was during the second session held in 1963, however, that Wojtyla really came to notice. On 23rd September, during early discussions on the Constitution of the Church *(Lumen Gentium)* he urged that the Church should be viewed as "People of God" before any discussion of the hierarchy was considered. In other words he was asking for a less clerical and more biblical approach to the Church's vision of itself. The implications of this for the theology of the laity were considerable and those who had dismissed all Polish bishops as arch-conservatives were astounded. Wojtyla's scholarship made him one of the principal architects of *Lumen Gentium*, a document which re-orientated the whole Church, away from the Church constructed as a monarchical pyramid, towards the form of a body in which everyone is responsible for the mission of the Church but each in his own way. The role of the layman is thus in the world where he actually is; it is there that he must build the Church.

In later discussions Wojtyla's profound awareness of the realities of the contemporary world experienced under an oppressive regime brought a sense of perspective to the Council. He insisted on the need for religious freedom for all religious groups, however embarrassing this might be for the Roman Catholic Church. The Church could only demand religious liberty in the face of hostility if it was prepared to concede it itself. Again, speaking on the subject of atheism, his first hand experience came to bear. Out-and-out condemnation, he said, only served to make further dialogue impossible. Discussion should start instead on the basis of a recognition that we are all involved on a common search in the midst of human experience. "Let us avoid moralizing, or the suggestion that we have a monopoly of the truth. One of the major defects of this draft is that in it the Church appears merely as an authoritarian institution". Because of his valuable contribution to the discussion on religious liberty, Wojtyla had been invited to join the mixed Commission which dealt with Schema XIII, a draft which was eventually to become *Gaudium et Spes*: the Constitution of the Church in the World of Today. In what may well now seem a petty argument about the wording of the title, it was Wojtyla who found the solution by defining it as a "pastoral" constitution, thereby emphasizing that it was concerned not so much with doctrine as with life – with contemporary problems such as war and peace, economic development and international organization and also, at the instigation of Wojtyla, with marriage and the family.

By December 1965, the Second Vatican Council was officially over and the bishops returned to their respective dioceses. It was a further seven years, however, before the documents were actually completed, and Wojtyla returned at regular intervals to Rome. Meanwhile, at home in Poland, he set about implementing the decisions of the Second Vatican Council. Liturgical changes such as the turning of the altar to face the people and the celebration of the Mass in the vernacular rather than in Latin, he, unlike Cardinal Wyszinski, accepted easily, but commitment to the spirit of the Council must go much deeper. As a Church leader, Wojtyla is demanding both of himself and of others. He has always recognized wholeheartedly the need for fidelity to the mission with which he has been entrusted, placing considerable weight on what he calls "the great discipline of the Church". Fidelity means respect for liturgical norms determined by Church authorities; love is the fountain which sustains and the climate in which we grow. Concepts such as the bond of collegiality which binds together the bishops "with Peter and under Peter" must be looked at in the spirit of love and accepted from the heart. What had been explicitly stated by the Council must be instantly put into practice and what had remained "implicit" would become evident with experiment and changing circumstances. In the light of all this and in order to further a full understanding of the Council's decrees, in 1972 Wojtyla set up a Synod involving a large number of clergy and laity to meet and pray together and discuss the draft texts. He also wrote, for the benefit of the synodal assemblies, a guide to the implementation of Vatican II, entitled "Foundations of Renewal".

⚜ ⚜ ⚜ ⚜ ⚜

It may come as a surprise to some to learn that Karol Wojtyla as bishop, archbishop and cardinal still found time to write. Even more surprising for many is the fact that he was still writing poetry. A talent for poetry and the need to give poetic expression to personal sensitivity in a young man deeply immersed in the study of language and literature is not so startling; the same need found in a Church leader profoundly committed to pastoral ministry, to the vicissitudes of Church-State relations within Poland and to the complexities of the Church's role in the world at large, is possibly more unusual. Yet it would seem that, for Wojtyla, writing poetry was a natural and continuing means of expression for an important aspect of his

personality, for his poetry appears to span a period from the mid-1940s to as late as 1975. It has been seen that even in his early years, Wojtyla's poems were not merely the sentimental outpourings of an emotional youth, and in the course of time his work developed powerfully until he emerged as what Boleslaw Taborski, another poet, has described as "among the major religious poets of our

At Monte Cassino, on the occasion of his 59th birthday, John Paul pays tribute to the Polish soldiers who died in May, 1944.

time". Taborski has referred to him as a "religious" poet. Neither the phraseology nor the imagery of Wojtyla's writings are overtly devotional or superficially "religious". Yet the connection between his poetry and his spiritual works is implicitly apparent. The pseudonym under which his works were published both in *Znak*, the monthly magazine of the movement of Catholic Intellectuals and in *Tygodnik Poswzechny*, their weekly newspaper, is in itself significant. Andrzej Jawien was the name of the hero in a famous pre-war novel, "The Sky in Flames" by Jan Parandowski. The title refers to the young hero's loss of faith, and the choice of pseudonym may well intimate the recognition that faith, in order to be strong, must first be tried and tested. In his poetry Wojtyla frequently takes as his starting point a religious or biblical theme and applies it to the contemporary world in a way which reflects a deeply felt compassion for humanity as a whole. "Profiles of a Cyrenean" for example, recounts how Simon was forced to carry the cross of Christ to Golgotha.

> "And then He comes. He lays his yoke
> on your back. You feel it, you tremble, you are awake."

Simon is not alone, for we are all of us Cyreneans

> "I know the Cyrenean's profile best,
> from every conceivable point of view."

We must all carry crosses – with which we do not wish to be burdened and against which we try to rebel – so the Cyrenean cycle pinpoints the everyday crosses of individuals in the contemporary world; a car factory worker, a worker from an armaments factory, a woman typing for eight hours a day, a girl whose heart has been broken, the man of emotion and the man of intellect:

> "How cramped are your notions, formulas, judgements
> always condensing yet hungry for content.
>
> Don't break down my defences, accept the human lot;
> each load must take the direction of thought."

Wojtyla's writings are a powerful witness to his fundamental Christian humanism. They are the poetry of one who has a sympathetic understanding of human emotions, of life, of children:

> "Growing unawares through love, of a sudden
> they've grown up, and hand in hand
> wander in crowds (their hearts caught like buds,
> profiles pale in the dusk)
> The pulse of mankind beats in their hearts."

but above all they are poems of ideas in which intangible truths are given concrete expression. In "Marble Floor", a poem which has recently provoked particular interest, Wojtyla meditates upon the floor of St. Peter's Basilica which becomes the symbolic representation of the role of the Pope.

> "Peter, you are the floor, that others
> may walk over you (not knowing
> where they go). You guide their steps
> so that spaces can be one in their eyes,
> and from them thought is born."

In addition to poetry Wojtyla has written countless essays, articles and plays. Dealing with a variety of subjects ranging from dramatic theory to detailed insights into human relationships, they all combine to proclaim the message, which he took as one of his main themes of the retreat for the Roman Curia – the words of St. Irenaeus: "The glory of God is that man should be fully alive". His books "The Acting Person", "Foundations of Renewal" and "Love and Responsibility" all emphasize the importance of human experience and of a positive relationship to the humanity and the dignity of others. They also advocate a sense of harmonious community as opposed to isolation. "Love and Responsibility" in particular, deals in detail with the theme of man as an individual, and the difficulties involved in the formation and development of personal relationships. It is a work of Catholic orthodoxy in its attempt to provide a rational justification for the Church's traditional teaching on sexual morality. Taking as its theme the love between man and woman, it advocates,

as do the documents of Vatican II, the love that is a mutual self-giving and not a mutual exploitation. The preoccupation with family life which occurs and recurs in Wojtyla's works is, it may be argued, the direct product of life in a society in which this was the only area where a sense of freedom from State directives could be retained, but then would not this same society make the recognition and proclamation of the dignity of man more difficult? The solution lies in the mystery of love that is at the base of all things. In his poem, "Reflection on Fatherhood", Wojtyla foresees the day when God will allow this world to crumble. "And everything else will then become unimportant and unessential, except the father, the child and love. And then also, looking at the simplest things, all of us will say: couldn't we have learned all this long ago? Was not all that always embedded at the bottom of everything that is?" (Excerpt translated by B. Taborski.)

In 1976 Wojtyla was invited by Pope Paul VI to conduct a retreat for the Holy Father and for the Roman Curia. He chose to center his sermons on the prophetic words spoken by Simeon on seeing the child Jesus: "Behold, he is set for the fall and the rising of many in Israel, and as a sign of contradiction" (Luke 2, 34). To Wojtyla the world today is the realization of Simeon's prediction: "If now – on the threshold of the last quarter-century before the second millennium, after the Second Vatican Council, and in the face of the terrible experiences the human family has undergone and is still undergoing – Jesus Christ is once again revealing himself to men as the light of the world, has he not also become at one and the same time that sign which, more than ever, men are resolved to oppose?" Such a world merely emphasizes the need for Christ, who in himself guarantees the essential profile of the "mystery of man". "Given our society today, in which falsity and hypocrisy reign supreme, public opinion is manipulated, consciences bludgeoned, apostasy is sometimes imposed by force and there is organized persecution of the faith – sometimes camouflaged but all the more terrible for that – the Christ who bore witness to the truth is more than ever the Christ for us: 'Christus propheta magnus'."

Skier, canoeist, mountaineer, actor, linguist; a man who was Professor of Ethics at Lublin and committed to a highly complex and carefully defined philosophy and yet was possessed of a faith which found its expression in such simple actions as the heading of his lecture notes with the initials J and M for Jesus and Mary; the intellectual who was capable of confronting Marxism at its highest level and of impressing the leading theologians of the Roman Catholic Church with the clarity of his thinking; the pastoral priest who regarded the Solway factory workers as some of his most treasured parishioners; the man of action and the man of prayer; a man who risked his life repeatedly during the Occupation and a poet whose works are a moving and glorious hymn to life; a patriot and a citizen of the world profoundly concerned with universal human rights – it is small wonder that in October 1978 a leading editorial article described the cardinals' choice as one displaying a "touch of imaginative rashness". The world, baffled by a series of apparent paradoxes, came to the cautious conclusion that John Paul II was a moderate progressive but not an innovator, but anticipated nevertheless a papacy such as had never before been witnessed. In Poland, people were delighted. Wojtyla's former housekeeper dismissed all question of paradox or complexity with the simple statement "He is a good man" and the Polish government added one more paradox by deciding, after some considerable discussion, to send a telegram of congratulations to the Vatican and at the same time contriving to tell the world that the new pope was the product of a good socialist state.

In the meantime, John Paul himself embarked upon his pontificate with a rhythm of work which was impressive, not least for the fact that he appeared to achieve it without rushing. On the morning of 17th October, he appeared as if untouched by the cold isolation of the "mountain", to deliver in characteristic tones the discourse which was to bring the conclave to its conclusion. It was a speech remarkable for its content, in that it had been prepared in so short a space of time, but to those who knew and understood the man, it was very much a confirmation of what had gone before. In it John Paul II committed himself unhesitatingly to the Second Vatican Council: "Before anything else, we wish to emphasize the continuing importance of the Second Vatican Ecumenic Council. To us this constitutes a formal obligation to see it executed with diligence". He went on to add: "First of all, we must become in tune with the Council, in order to apply in practice what the Council has stated emphatically and to reaffirm that which one usually understands to be implicit, in the light of experiments undertaken since that time and the demands created by new circumstances". Here, to those radicals who hoped to find it, was some scope for "reinterpretation" of the truth. In the areas in which many were hoping for innovation, such as those of women priests, abortion and contraception, Pope John Paul II did not at this stage commit himself. He did, however, call for close examination of the subject of collegiality, a doctrine to which he intended to adhere: "Most particularly we do encourage an examination of the principle of collegiality, to become more deeply aware of it, and at the same time to enable us to do our duty with greater watchfulness. Collegiality intimately connects the bishops with the successor to Peter and unites them among themselves. It allows them to bring the light of the gospel to the world, to sanctify it through the avenues of grace the Church extends and to assume leadership with a shepherd's care towards all the people of God. Collegiality also means the creation of organizations, partly new ones, partly existing ones, but adapted to today's needs."

The homily delivered on the death of John Paul I had reminded those present that, in a sense, Christ always asks of the successor to St. Peter the same question delivered to Simon Peter: "Do you love me more than

His Holiness at Monte Cassino.

others?" The call to papal authority invariably includes a call to greater love, and so in his very first address as pope, John Paul II chose in all humility to respond to that question: "With St. Paul we repeat: 'For the love of Christ

restraineth us'. Right from the beginning we wish to see our ministry as a service of love, this will permeate all our actions." John Paul's first address was characteristic in many ways: in its profession of loyalty to the Second Vatican Council, in its approach to collegiality, in its expressed intention to continue the steps already taken

John Paul has a special smile for children in one of the poorer suburbs of Rome.

towards ecumenism, in its reference to the Virgin Mary whose name many years earlier, together with the words *Totus Tuus* (all thine), he had inscribed on his heart and on his coat of arms, and in the special greetings he remembered to include for Poland, *semper fidelis*. Most characteristic of all, however, was his resolve to examine and to undertake the Petrine ministry in the light of its threefold scriptural basis, and in the spirit of that love which is the source that nourishes and the climate in which one grows.

John Paul II's "service of love" began with an energy and a disregard for protocol which was to disconcert some within the Vatican but which was to endear him to many outside it. It is not usual for a newly elected pope to leave the Vatican before he is officially inaugurated but on the first evening after the papal election, John Paul had already "escaped". His compatriot and friend Monsignor Andrea Deskur had suffered a heart attack and been admitted to the Gremelli Hospital four days previously, and so the Pope strode determinedly out of the Vatican to visit the sick man. After a brief, informal audience with assembled hospital staff, John Paul was on the point of leaving without giving his blessing. A whispered reminder was greeted with a smile. "I still have to learn how to behave as pope", he admitted. Yet the addresses delivered in the short space of time preceding the inauguration ceremony displayed no lack of confidence. His dealings with the cardinals, with the press and with the diplomatic corps, revealed instead an air of unpretentious self-assurance and ability.

The "inauguration of John Paul II's ministry as supreme pastor" took place on the mild autumnal morning of Sunday, 22nd October. Attended by a crowd of 300,000 people, among them dignitaries ranging from the Archbishop of Canterbury to the Polish Head of State, the ceremony amounted to what can only be described as a non-triumphalistic triumph. Like his predecessor, John Paul II chose not to be crowned with the papal tiara but rather to be invested with a pallium. This long woollen band has been presented to metropolitan archbishops of both East and West since the fourth century. It is made of lamb's wool given to the pope on the feast of St. Agnes, and is therefore linked with pastoral care. It is placed on the shoulders like a yoke and is in this way a reminder that the service of a Christian is not easy but that, with the help of the Lord, it is light. It is also presented to the metropolitan and to the pope as coming "from the tomb of St. Peter": thus stewardship in the church is linked with the founding apostle. Finally, it is a reminder that the successor to Peter is also bishop of Rome. It was clothed in this garment, steeped in the symbolism of humility, that John Paul II received the homage of the individual cardinals. To the accompaniment of the singing of the text "Thou art Peter, and upon this rock I will build my Church" they came forward one by one to kneel and kiss the Fisherman's ring. Among the first in line was the staunch old Polish patriot, Cardinal Wyszinski, who only a few days previously as Primate of Poland had been Wojtyla's superior. Now the old warrior knelt to make his obeisance, only to be forestalled by his compatriot. Raising the Cardinal carefully to his feet the Pope embraced him three times in truly Polish fashion, then kissed his hand. In Poland, the thousands gathered round television screens to watch the first Mass ever to be shown on Polish television, wept openly. In Rome, John Paul II moved slowly to the altar to celebrate his first

In Poland, the inauguration of the Polish Pope was the first Mass ever to be shown on television.

pontifical Mass. Before the staring eyes of the omnipresent television cameras he raised the ornate golden chalice, and as he did so, centuries of papal grandeur seemed to many to slip away, leaving only the simplest of acts – that of a man worshipping his creator.

The Pope's homily took as its text: "Thou art the Christ, the Son of the living God" (Matthew 16:15). He saw his role as rock-apostle as that of proclaiming the essential faith of Peter, of placing himself in a position of subordination to the Gospels. His authority must be of the kind that expresses itself not in the exercise of power, but in love and truth and so, watched by countless millions of people all over the world, he uttered an ardent and humble prayer: "Christ, allow me to be and remain a servant of your unique power, a servant of your power who is filled with gentleness, a servant of your endless power, or rather, a servant of your servants". Then came the ringing appeal "Open wide the doors for Christ. To his saving power open the boundaries of states, economic and political systems, the vast fields of culture, civilization and development. Do not be afraid. Christ knows what is in man: He alone knows it". Strangely this plea was left untranslated on Polish television. The rest of the world heard it however. They heard also the greetings he added in English, French, German, Spanish, Portuguese, Ukrainian, Russian and Czech, and watched as he insisted

John Paul celebrates a Mass in a Roman suburb.

on mingling with the crowd after the ceremony was over. They were left with a sense of having encountered, possibly for the first time, a man of a great faith, of great strength and yet of great humility.

꧁ ꧁ ꧁ ꧁ ꧁

The danger of great expectations is always that their actual realization may prove an anticlimax. As far as the pontificate of John Paul II is concerned, however, it may be said with considerable justification that the reality has proved as interesting as the speculation which accompanied his election. Certainly it has not been a dull pontificate to date and shows no sign of becoming one. John Paul II has shown in his first year as pope, perhaps more effectively than any of his predecessors, that popes are not merely stereotyped figures dressed in white, who make occasional appearances on distant balconies and utter ceremonial platitudes. If the cardinals were looking for a pastoral pope – a people's pope – their choice has been more than vindicated. From the very first John Paul II made his refusal to be separated from his people by papal etiquette readily apparent. From the moment when, after the inauguration mass, he strode vigorously down to a group of Poles and insisted on greeting personally a number of cripples in wheelchairs, he has been a constant source of nervous anxiety to Mgr. Virgilio Noé, papal master of ceremonies. As the Tablet's correspondent in Rome put it, his behaviour is likely "to give healthy nightmares to protocol slaves until they either fade away or adjust themselves." Protocol prelates have given up laying protective hands on the Pope's arm and saying "basta" to indicate that he has talked for long enough to one individual and it is time to move on. The Holy Father merely shrugged their hands off with disconcerting ease and continued talking. In vain Vatican officials tried to induce him to walk rapidly through the audiences, or to allow himself to be carried in his gestatorial chair. Prelates hurrying him forward found themselves firmly restrained by a muscular papal arm and the chair was simply ignored. So it is that the journey from the door of St. Peter's to the chair at the altar, from which he talks during his overcrowded general audiences takes John Paul more than half an hour. Paul VI covered the same ground in an estimated three minutes.

John Paul has gone to considerable trouble to quieten any potential discontent among Italians. In Italy, he always speaks Italian and he has let it be generally known that he is only the Pope because he is Bishop of Rome. He has held special audiences for Roman priests, nuns and seminarians, and done everything within his power to fulfil the intention expressed early in his pontificate: "I intend to do something every Sunday for the diocese." On Sunday 29th October, the Pope went by helicopter to visit the shrine of Mentorella, some thirty miles outside Rome, the site of a twelfth century statue presided over by a community of Polish monks. The visit marked the beginning of papal activity, in and around Rome, such as had never before been experienced. Within a few weeks this foreign pope had visited two shrines; taken possession of St. John Lateran, the Bishop of Rome's basilica; visited one of the suburbs of Rome; spent some time at the papal residence at Castelgandolfo; celebrated Mass in Santa Maria Maggiore, the largest basilica dedicated to the Virgin; laid a wreath at the statue of the Virgin Mary off the Spanish Steps, and held a public meeting with the Communist Mayor of Rome, Giulio Carlo Argan. Within days John Paul II was being greeted everywhere with enthusiastic cheers and cries of *"Viva il Papa"* which were heartfelt. "At last", was the general feeling, "we have a Bishop of Rome."

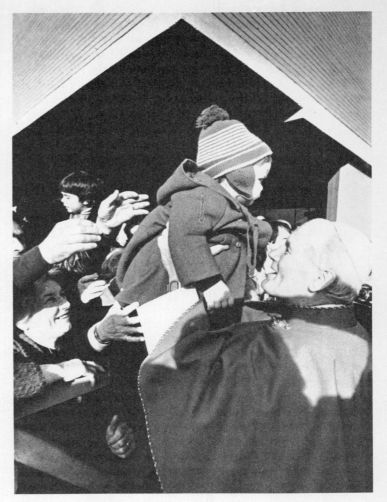

John Paul II, the "pastoral pope".

On 25th February, 1979, in St Peter's, John Paul conducted a marriage service for Vittoria Ianni and Mario Maltese.

"Pastoral" has continued to be an important word in the ministry of Wojtyla. It is not for nothing that he referred to the mission of Peter as that of "pastoral responsibility for the entire church". In Rome he has conducted a wedding for a road-sweeper's daughter, baptised a British baby and above all he has not been afraid to abandon the ceremonial trappings of the papacy to draw nearer to the people for whom he feels joyously responsible. In August 1979, this most cheerfully unconventional of popes tramped through 12 inches of snow across a mountain top to bless a 6 foot bronze Madonna, a tribute to the bravery of Alpine women. With a smile that threatened to melt the snow, and wearing a peaked white fur cap, a white windjacket and red ski boots, he stood on an icy plateau at 9,792 feet and spread out his arms to welcome a congregation of at least

seven hundred people. It is gestures of this kind which have won him the hearts of the Italian people and indeed the hearts of the world at large. In his relatively short time as Pope, John Paul II has already kissed the ground of the Dominican Republic, Mexico, Poland, Ireland and the U.S.A. In each of these places he has been accompanied throughout his visit by enormous crowds, responding with enthusiasm to the warmth and the concentration which he brings to everything he does, and in each of these places he has made it clear that to him crowds are not merely crowds, but collections of individuals, important in their own right. He has walked among them, laughed with them, sung with them, wept with them, kissed their children – and all this in a way that, even in this cynical world, has not compromised his image as a man of God.

On 21st October, 1978, the newly elected pope held a meeting for two thousand journalists.

However splendid the trappings of each state visit, John Paul succeeds in transforming his journeys into pilgrimages – in Mexico, to our Lady of Guadelupe; in Poland to the revered Black Madonna of Jasna Gora. In Ireland he came as a "pilgrim for Christ", following in the footsteps of Saint Patrick. The highlight of his pastoral visit was his devotion at the shrine of Mary, Queen of Ireland, in Knock. These tributes are not merely lipservice paid to Catholic Mariology, but rather the product of a profound faith and spirituality which somehow commands recognition. When John Paul II kneels to pray, whether it be before the barbed wire fences of Auschwitz, or in the majestic splendor of St. Patrick's Cathedral in New York, the most loquacious voices of the materialism he so ardently condemns, fall silent.

John Paul has been prepared to bare his soul to the world. On the day before his inauguration he held a meeting for two thousand journalists in the Hall of Benedictions, and without hesitation changed the policy of Vatican dealings with the media, at a single stroke. The Vatican Press Office had previously been described as making "Kremlin spokesmen seem like chatty salesmen." The Polish Pope, predictably in the light of his fight for Church access to the media in Poland, and of his admiration for freedom of expression experienced during a visit to the United States in 1969, now proclaimed: "It is my emphatic wish that religious reporters have access to the necessary help from the authorized ecclesiastical departments. The latter must receive them with every respect for their convictions and their position." After his set piece John Paul II moved through the Hall of Benedictions and, to the horror of those Vatican Officials who had anticipated that a non-Italian pope would be nervous and manipulable, proceeded to answer questions from individual groups of journalists. This meeting was to set the tone of his whole approach to the press. It is rare that he completes a flight without spending some considerable time talking to the numerous journalists who accompany him on his journeys. Remarkably, he has survived this "exposure" to emerge as a spiritual leader, universally acknowledged to be a "good man", a "man of love".

In a world where the motives of a politician embracing a child are immediately suspect, there is a temptation to regard the "good man" who does the same thing with transparent sincerity, as naive. There are those who have applied the principle that goodness precludes shrewdness to John Paul's "service of love", but to do so is to ignore his past achievements and to underestimate the intellect which undoubtedly functions as effectively as his heart. The man who impulsively envelops people in his huge and powerful bearhug, is, in his business office, anything but impulsive, and it is not for nothing that so many of the world's ecclesiastical and political leaders have admired his insight into world affairs. Those who interpreted his slowness to make new appointments or confirm already existing ones in the Vatican hierarchy as an irresponsible preoccupation with getting to know his diocese are already biting their tongues, for now John Paul has the hierarchy completely under control. In March, the death of Cardinal Villot, the Secretary of State he inherited from his predecessor, gave the Pope, whose preoccupation with human rights is a deep-rooted conviction stemming, as has been seen, not only from personal experience but also from the long-standing traditions of his nation, the opportunity to recast the higher échelons of his government according to his own notions. His new Secretary of State, Cardinal Agostino Casaroli, has been involved in the East-West détente policy, and the global human rights campaign. Archbishop Achille Silverstrini, who has taken

In November, 1978 John Paul visited Assisi to pray to St. Francis and to bless the Franciscan fathers.

over the foreign affairs portfolio, was deeply involved in the Helsinki Declaration on religious liberty and all the resultant moves in the human rights field. The post of *sostituto* (deputy) has gone to Archbishop Eduardo Martinez Somalo, a Spaniard with a detailed knowledge of the human rights movement in Latin America, and the third foreign affairs post is held by Mgr. Andryss Backio, a Lithuanian, in charge of Soviet territories. Together they all point towards human rights as the main diplomatic thrust of the Church's activities.

The principle underlying the Pope's global strategy is that ultimately, totalitarian regimes, of any kind or political complexion, are incompatible with human rights. If they deny such basic rights, they can be legitimately challenged, particularly by the Church. If, on the other hand, they concede them, even in part, they are set on a course of self-destruction. To become the effective champion of human rights, the Church must be seen to be even-handed, as between Communist and capitalist regimes, and must be seen to uphold religious freedom and atheist freedom, even where it conflicts with her own interests. Subject to these two qualifications, John Paul, and with him the Roman Catholic Church, is committed absolutely to the cause of human freedom as expressed in the Rights of Man.

In Warsaw, the Pope kneels to pray before the tomb of the unknown soldier.

Viewed within the broad framework of this strategy, the man who has expressed the intention of visiting every major Catholic population center in the world, does not emerge quite as the simple pilgrim riding unawares on a wave of religious fervor engendered by his own impressive personality. John Paul's first overseas visit was made with the intention of attending the bishops' conference of Latin America in Puebla, Mexico. Latin America now includes the largest concentration of Roman Catholics; it is also the area where the church is under the most pressure to enter the political arena and embrace the "theology of liberation". The Pope's major speech at Puebla was a masterpiece of diplomacy which brought comfort to both Left and Right wings of the Church. It was also the direct product of his humanism. In it, he dismissed "liberation theology" as a "false reinterpretation" of the Gospel. Christ was not "a political figure, a revolutionary, the subversive man from Nazareth". To interpret the Kingdom of God as mere political liberation was to empty it of its richness. The Church did not need an ideological system to inspire her, her own teachings compelled her "to love, defend and take part in the liberation of man: at the very center of the message of which she is guardian and herald, she stands for brotherhood, justice and peace – she is against all forms of domination, slavery, discrimination, violence,

attacks on religious liberty, aggression against man – everything which is against life". The Church must preach "to transform hearts and humanize the political and economic systems . . . to bring about liberation in its internal and deepest meaning."

The objective of the Church, which holds the truth concerning the nobility of man "is to bring up the complete man who, guided by truth, becomes a mature member of society" . . . "A human person cannot develop and perfect himself apart from the search for the common welfare." This was the case for freedom which John Paul took with him to his native Poland in June. Religious freedom is an inalienable human right and the Church will fight any organization which denies it, in theory or in practice. Ultimately, the primary target of the new Vatican policy must be the Soviet empire. No self-respecting Pole, least of all a passionate libertarian like John Paul II, can admit the permanency of the Soviet occupation of Eastern Europe. An article written by John Paul for the Italian magazine *Vita e Pensiero* shortly before his election, states vehemently that the EEC concept of "Europe" is incomplete – the Iron Curtain is a detestable and artificial, and therefore impermanent, division of a culture. The Pope believes that religion, armed with the human rights issue, can eventually undermine the Soviet empire from within, and so he will maintain the pressure he has already exerted on the regime in Poland – he intends to return there in 1982 for the 600th anniversary of the shrine of Czestochowa. He also intends to persuade the Communist authorities to allow him to visit Hungary and Czechoslovakia and the Catholic communities in Lithuania and the Ukraine.

There is no doubt also that reunion with the Orthodox East is high on the list of John Paul's priorities. He has already set up his own lines of communication with the Patriarchate in Moscow, and receives numerous discreet visits from Athens, Constantinople and other parts of the Orthodox world. The Pope's recently announced journey to Turkey is also expected to produce concrete results in accelerating the quest for unity between the Roman Catholic and the Orthodox Church. The motive behind the quest, it may be suggested, lies not only in the interests of ecumenism but also in the furtherance of human rights. If Rome and Orthodoxy were to heal their schism, the Soviet state-sponsored church structures would collapse, and the struggle for religious rights in Russia would at last be brought into the open.

The campaign for human rights does not, however, operate solely on the "other" side of the Curtain. On the 29th September, John Paul II became the first Pope to set foot in Ireland. There were those who imagined that he saw Ireland and Poland as victims as a common predicament, and John Paul was doubtless aware of the tendency to cast Britain and Russia in the same oppressive role, but as a Pole he was aware too, of the dangers of such an analogy. No Pole can easily see Britain, the nation which remained the friend and ally of a conquered and occupied Poland, as an enemy of human rights. John Paul's message to Ireland was that violence and terrorism had no part to play in human rights activity: "Violence is a lie, for it goes against the truth of our faith, the truth of our humanity. Violence destroys what it claims to defend: the dignity, the life, the freedom of human beings. Violence is a crime against humanity, for it destroys the very fabric of society." To deprive an individual of his life is to make the worst possible assault on his human rights. A British soldier and a policeman in the RUC have human rights like everybody else.

With such a prelude, it goes almost without saying that John Paul's main theme, in his address to the United

Nations Assembly in America, proclaimed that peace is threatened by any violation of human rights. The United Nations could fulfil its role as peace-keeper only if it consistently applied its own 1948 Universal Declaration of Human Rights. Before a silent assembly of delegates, some of whom were undoubtedly embarrassed or irritated, the Pope denounced the arms race: "The continual preparations for war . . . mean taking the risk that some time, somewhere, somehow, someone can set in motion the terrible mechanism of general destruction." Then with unfaltering conviction he went on to pray that "every kind of concentration camp anywhere on earth may once and for all be done away with", condemning outright "the various kinds of torture and oppression, either physical or moral, carried out . . . under the pretext of internal "security" or the need to preserve an apparent peace".

Those who feared that John Paul might be distracted from the planning of a long term world policy need not have worried. The violence may not have ceased in Ireland, but the Pope's visit left behind it an atmosphere of renewed hope, and as far as the central human rights crusade is concerned, the salutary impact of this courageous, rigorous, and relentless man on the world scene is in the fullest sense of the word, immeasureable.

The passion for freedom expressed in a plea for human rights is an issue which the Church as a whole can applaud, although its members may well be at variance over the methods by which such freedom should be achieved. Another similar issue is that of ecumenism – an objective generally acknowledged to be "a good thing" and one which John Paul has shown his intention of furthering. He has done so largely by the stress on collegiality. One of the principal stumbling blocks to unity between the Roman Catholic Church and, for example, the Anglican Church or the United States Episcopalian Church, had been the interpretation of the First Vatican Council of the role of the pope. Vatican II's insight that the Petrine ministry does not exist in isolation reduced that stumbling block considerably. The pope is not now seen over against, or above his brother bishops but as one of

The Holy Father responds to the welcome of President Jimmy Carter at the White House in Washington.

them. His special role is not in any way diminished. He still has "the solicitude of all the Churches" but he does not bear the burden alone. The requirement to other Church leaders to recognize the pope as "first among equals" is not so contentious, and the Archbishop of Canterbury, Dr. Coggan, has agreed that on historical grounds he would accept that the pope was first among

Shortly after his inauguration at the Marian Shrine of Mentarella pilgrims and posters await the arrival of the Pope.

equals. The way is now open for some of the divisions between Christians to be healed.

John Paul II has gone to great lengths to demonstrate that he is not a monarch in the sense that former popes were, even to the degree that Paul VI was. In an attempt to solve a number of problems, among them the critical financial state of the Vatican, in November 1979 the Pope called for an extraordinary meeting of 129 Cardinals, (some of them too old to vote in the conclave), to examine the Church's role in the modern world. The running of the meeting he left to three Cardinals, in an effort to underline the importance of the Princes of the Church. The principle of collegiality must prevail, but it is interesting to note that those who work in conjunction with him have little doubt that he would be prepared to brandish the Keys of Peter to devastating effect should he consider it necessary. Pope John Paul II comes, after all, from a tradition where the value of authority is greatly respected.

At the time of his election there were some who feared that a Polish pope might have difficulty in adjusting to Western secular mentality; that despite the talk of collegiality there was a danger of the Roman Catholic Church becoming more authoritarian. Certainly the latter prediction has proved in some ways to be justified. In April the Vatican congregation for the doctrine of the faith condemned a book by a French Dominican as contrary to Catholic teaching – it was the first such proscription in ten years. It may be suggested, however, that John Paul's failure to adapt to 'Western secular mentality' is not so much because of his inability to do so but rather because of a deliberate rejection of what he sees as threatening the foundation of it, namely the fact that "even where Christ is accepted there is at the same time opposition to the full truth of his Person, his mission and his Gospel". In his retreat on the theme of the "Sign of Contradiction" Cardinal Wojtyla outlined this danger: "There is a desire to 're-shape' him, to adapt him to suit mankind in this era of progress and make him fit in with the program of modern civilization – which is a program of consumerism and not of transcendental ends. There is opposition to him from those standpoints, and the truth proclaimed and recorded in his name is not tolerated (cf Acts 4, 10, 12, 18). This opposition to Christ which goes hand-in-hand with paying him lip-service – and it is to be found also among those who call themselves his disciples – is particularly symptomatic of our own times". This is the kind of thinking which lies at the heart of Pope John Paul's 'conservatism'.

The man whose self-confident celebration of his own vocation is so apparent and so reassuring has shown no relaxation on the status of priests, religious or nuns. One of his first actions as Pope was to stop the laicization of priests and others who wished to return to lay life. The concept of sacrifice for one's beliefs is understandably deep-rooted; the ideal of Maksymilian Kolbe walks ever before him. To those priests who wished to lift the 1500 years old ban on marriage, said by some to be one of the main causes for the steady defection of priests from the ministry, his reply was the firm reminder that "We must retain the sense of our unique vocation. . . We are in the world but we are not worldly." To John Paul the reason for the defection is a "crisis of identity"; the solution lies in the security offered only by solid spirituality and not in encouraging those who have taken vows of obedience and chastity in their "refusal to be tested".

Not surprisingly another mark of Wojtyla's papacy has been a halting of the tide of sexual permissiveness which at one time threatened to engulf even Roman Catholicism. The Vatican and United States ecclesiastical authorities are now disowning the notorious "Human Sexuality: New Directions in Catholic Thought", "A Study commissioned by the Catholic Theological Society of America". The report takes a very liberal attitude towards fetishism, transvestism, "sex clinics", sex-change operations, sex-therapy, pornography, fornication for "divorced singles", "involuntary singles" and widows, and towards homosexual acts. For John Paul this kind of activity is a degradation of the human personality and an assault on man's dignity. Sexual permissiveness is a contradiction of his concept of human rights, for it is based upon a separation between love and sex and the responsibility which is part of love. Like the concentration camps of Auschwitz, it reduces the human body to the status of an object. Similarly, it is difficult to imagine how this pope could accept the radical interference with human biology involved in the contraceptive pill.

The Pope made his clearest rejection of artificial birth control since his election to the papacy in Chicago during his October visit to America. With characteristic deftness he praised 350 American bishops for their support of the controversial encyclical letter of Pope Paul VI, *Humanae Vitae* (of human life) which spelled out the prohibition. He said that the bishops themselves had, in a pastoral letter, rightly spoken against both the ideology of contraception and contraceptive acts. He also reaffirmed "the right to life and the inviolability of every human life, including the life of unborn children" and endorsed the view that euthanasia – or mercy killing – was a "grave moral evil". It was an announcement which was entirely consistent with his earlier teachings (some well-informed Church sources have suggested that Wojtyla's "Love and Responsibility" was one of the prime inspirations for Paul VI's "*Humanae Vitae*"), and with his vision of the family which "carries with it the most fundamental values of mankind" as the archetypal and natural expression of human solidarity. It was also the direct product not, as some would claim, of his inexperience of such matters as a committed celibate, but rather of his first-hand pastoral experience in Poland. During his years in Kraków he had founded a Family Institute and placed in charge of it a gifted woman psychiatrist, a survivor of Ravensbruck, who had served as guinea-pig for numerous hideous medical experiments. Through work in the Institute Wojtyla acquired a wide knowledge of divorce, alcoholism, wife-beating, poverty and sexual problems. His decisions on contraception and abortion arise not from an obliviousness to human problems but at least in part from a compassionate desire to protect the sanctity of the family unit from threats which he cannot help seeing as not dissimilar to the "operations" conducted in Nazi camps.

This was small comfort, however, for the increasing number of Roman Catholics who had hoped for a more liberal approach to sexual matters. Many were bitterly disappointed and yet, miraculously, the crowds continued to cheer. In Philadelphia the Pope closed the door to women in the priesthood in a reaffirmation of "the prophetic tradition". Some among his listeners received the news stony-faced but, with one or two exceptions among the Women's Liberation Movement, they joined enthusiastically in the rousing ovation which accompanied John Paul's departure. The Pope attacked the materialism of American society and hundreds of thousands of Americans – Catholics and non-Catholics, religious and atheists, applauded. He left America as he had left Mexico, Poland and Ireland and as he would return to Italy – to the sound of cries of joy and affection.

Inevitably the fact that so many express love and respect for the man while suggesting the impossibility of applying some of his teachings, more obviously those on contraception, to their own lives, provokes the question of whether the enthusiasm which greets his every move is merely a personality cult. In his address *Urbi et Orbi* at the conclusion of the conclave, John Paul stated with great determination: "Our own life, which so unexpectedly brought us to apostolic service, has scant value. Our personality, we wish to emphasize, must vanish through the heavy task we are called upon to perform." But has it and indeed should it? John Paul's charisma has earned him the nickname of "Superstar". One banner among the multitude that fly in the crowds assembled in St. Peter's Square recently greeted him as "the John Travolta of the Holy Spirit", and like John Travolta he too has been involved in the "pop scene". Shortly after his election, the "Wojtyla Disco Dance" heralded him with the somewhat dubious but no doubt well intentioned eulogy: "He's the groove, he's the man, the new pope in the Vatican". Needless to say, the Vatican after some hesitation, banned it. This was not quite the sort of "Superstar" they had in mind. Yet the personality is impressive. It is in no way to detract from the sincerity of John Paul to suggest that his dramatic training has shown him how most effectively to convey what he himself sincerely believes. He has a perfect sense of dramatic timing and of how best to employ a fascinating baritone voice, but over and above all this he is transparently a man in whom the four vital functions of body, mind, heart and soul are perfectly balanced. He has an easy and effective relationship with the physical, he has a first class rational mind, he has a real and in no way sentimental sense of compassion and a profound awareness of the spiritual, the transcendant dimension of all existence. This is what makes John Paul II so impressive. Like Christ his master he is a symbol of the fully-developed man, a symbol of something which every man must strive to become – which is why he constantly exhorts all men to become "kings" in their own inner kingdom.

The following of such a personality can only surely be for the good. Just as John Paul's papacy cannot really be divorced from the life that laid the foundation for it, so the personality cannot be divorced from the values which have shaped it, and to which it in turn is committed. Does the respect for such a personality point to a deep-rooted and enduring recognition of values much older than consumerism, and to a confirmation of Cardinal Confalinieri's assertion that what drew the crowds was a deep hunger for the nourishment of solid spirituality? Time alone can tell. One thing is certain. The imprint of conquered suffering on Wojtyla's face at rest, and the love which radiates from his ready smile, has restored to the splendor of the See of Peter, the ancient figure of the suffering servant. It is a figure which has been almost lost to the affluence of Western Europe and of North America but it is one which best bears witness to the spirit of Jesus Christ.

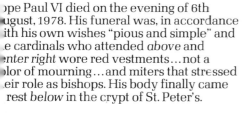

ope Paul VI died on the evening of 6th
ugust, 1978. His funeral was, in accordance
ith his own wishes "pious and simple" and
e cardinals who attended *above* and
enter right wore red vestments…not a
olor of mourning…and miters that stressed
eir role as bishops. His body finally came
rest *below* in the crypt of St. Peter's.

eft: In Kraków, Cardinal Wojtyla celebrated
Requiem Mass for the pope whom he had
ved and respected.
ar left: Cardinal Wojtyla and Cardinal
yszinski photographed in Rome before the
ugust conclave.
bove right: John Paul I, the man whose
irty-three day pontificate was so abruptly
oncluded.
elow right: The body of John Paul I lying in
ate in St. Peter's.

While the body of John Paul I lay in St. Peter's *left*, an apparently endless procession of mourners filed past, many of them weeping openly.

For the second time in less than two months the college of cardinals assembled in Rome, among them Cardinal Ursi *top*, Cardinal Pironio *above* and Cardinal Colombo *below*. Once more the Mass 'for electing the pope' was held *above right*, and once more the doors of the Sistine Chapel were sealed on the 111 cardinals, to ensure the secrecy of the conclave *center and below right*.

Seven times the smoke rising from the famous chimney in a cornice of St. Peter's turned slowly black, indicating to the crowd waiting in the square below that no decision had been reached, but at 6.18 pm on 16th October, as the smoke began to rise again *below*, it was indisputably white.

When the new pope appeared for the first time before the world *above* and *left*, it was to break with tradition. Before giving the customary Latin benediction *urbi et orbi*, he chose first to speak in Italian, thereby winning the hearts of the Roman crowd.

The inauguration of John Paul II on 22nd October, 1978 was attended by numerous heads of state, diplomats and foreign dignitaries. Many among the colorful congregation came in national dress, including groups from Poland who flocked with great pride and affection to witness the inauguration of the first Slav pope. Characteristically the Pope had asked that the ceremony be held at ten rather than later in the day, in order to avoid keeping the Italian fans from their televised football match in the afternoon.

Having received the pallium as a sign that he is bishop of Rome, the Pope accepted the homage of the cardinals in the ancient ceremony of the *obbedienza*, during which the cardinals kneel and kiss the Fisherman's ring and receive from him the kiss of peace. Then followed the Mass, during which the Pope prayed to God that he might worthily perform his duties as Vicar of Christ.

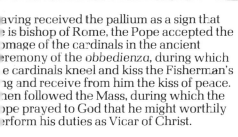

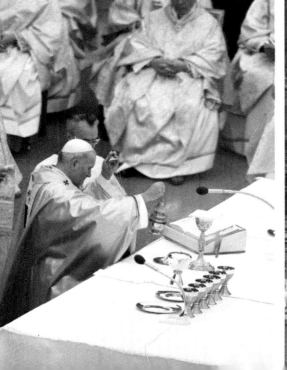

aving concluded the Mass, John Paul
ingled with the 250,000 people assembled
St. Peter's Square. Millions of people too,
d watched the live transmission of the
rvice on television sets throughout the
orld.

is inauguration was greeted with the
nthusiasm that was to follow him on the
any visits that he was soon to make
roughout Italy.

hn Paul II began his 'ministry of love' as he tended it to continue. In his first speech to urnalists *below*, he assured them: "You can unt on my understanding and I permit yself to expect the same from you" and, as defiance of protocol, he walked among e crowd, the same 'understanding' was erywhere apparent.

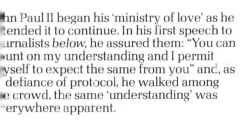

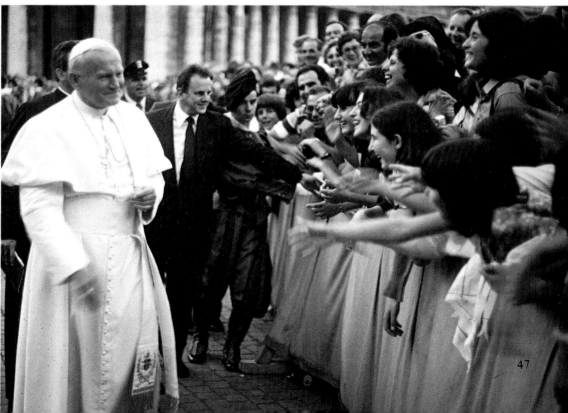

47

The life of John Paul II bears constant witness to his reverence for the dignity of man as a revelation of the 'mystery of Christ'. He has always made time for people and Vatican officials were initially disconcerted by his refusal to be separated from the surrounding crowds.

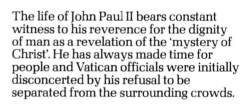

On 25th January, 1979 the Pope made his first journey outside Italy since becoming Pontiff. En route to Mexico, where he was to take part in the third international meeting of the Bishops' Conference of Latin America, he visited the Dominican Republic and was received with overwhelming exuberance.

52

53

Vast crowds gathered in Independence Square to attend an open-air Mass celebrated by Pope John Paul II on the following day, and before leaving for Mexico His Holiness was also able to meet and talk with President Guzman *below right*.

For the Pope, who is renowned for the fact that he seldom stops reading or writing, even in the back of a car, a 'plane journey *above* provides an opportunity to work or to meet with journalists.

Even a dawn earthquake could not halt the swarming pilgrimage to greet him in Mexico. The reception at the airport was so tumultuous that John Paul II could not reach microphones for an arrival speech and it took some considerable time to gain the open, truck-like vehicle that was to take him into the city.

At least 5 million people packed into Mexico City to see the Pope, who won them over shortly after his arrival by accepting a proffered Mexican hat and clapping it onto his head. Riding through the crowds he scored a symbolic victory in a country which is officially anti-clerical and the only one in Latin America to shun links with the Vatican.

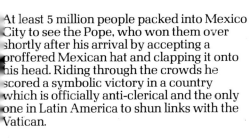

Mexico City's huge central square was packed for the Pontifical Mass which John Paul celebrated on the day of his arrival. So too, were the surroundings of the Shrine of Our Lady of Guadalupe *above*, which lies twenty minutes outside the city and which the Pope was also to visit.

Right: Pope John Paul II at Oaxaca.

60

Despite his expressed intention not to do so, President Jose Lopez Portillo did go to the airport to meet the Pope and when, on 29th January, John Paul flew the 300 miles to Oaxaca, it was in the president's 'plane. There half a million Roman Catholic Indians, many of them colorfully dressed in traditional costumes, were waiting to catch a glimpse of the Holy Father.

The packed streets of Mexico were festooned with flowers and portraits of the Pope for the duration of his visit and every public appearance he made was greeted with delighted enthusiasm.

Below: On 30th January the Pope paid a brief visit by helicopter to Santa Cecilia.

The reception throughout John Paul II's time in Mexico had been unquestionably warm and while his essentially conservative views expressed to the Conference of Latin American Bishops had left some uneasy feeling within the Church, it was clearly apparent that to the people at large, his visit had done much to dispel half a century of bitterness.

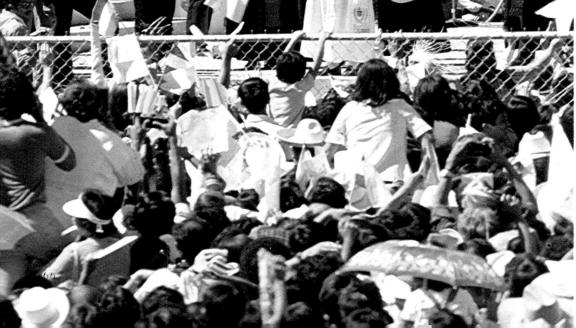

On Good Friday, almost exactly six months after his election, the Pope walked along a route marked by the Stations of the Cross, himself bearing a cross, from the Colosseum to the terrace of the Temple of Venus on the Palatine Hill.

The meditation and prayers at the Stations of the Cross formed part of the Easter celebrations, in the course of which John Paul II made an impassioned appeal for world peace.

69

On 2nd June, 1979 Pope John Paul II returned to his native land as the first Roman Catholic Pontiff ever to visit a communist country. The occasion was striking evidence that Poland is a land where two powerful ideologies have to some extent accepted the need for peaceful coexistence; it was also the homecoming of a dedicated patriot and, as the Pope stepped from his papel Boeing 727 at Okecie military airport to be greeted by Poland's Primate, Cardinal Wyszinski, it was a moment of great joy and profound emotion. For members of the Roman Catholic Church in particular, his visit was a source of great encouragement.

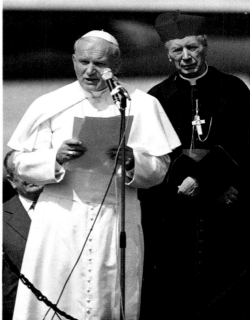

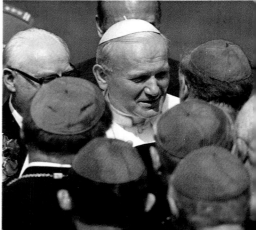

BŁ.RADZYM GAUDENTY PIĘCIU BRACI POLSKIC
YKT BŁ.BOGUMIŁ ŚW.STANISŁAW SZCZEPA
A BŁ.KINGA BŁ.JOLANTA ŚW.JACEK OD

A human tidal wave appeared to converge on Warsaw, to line the motorcade route from the airport into the city and when, during the afternoon, the Pope celebrated an open-air Mass before the Tomb of the Unknown Soldier in Victory Square, it was for a crowd of more than 250,000 people.

Paradoxically, approximately 90 percent of the population of this communist-ruled country are practicing Roman Catholics. It is small wonder then, that the state's attempts to prevent too obvious an outpouring of joy, failed miserably. The Pope's return meant a reunion with fellow churchmen. Above all, however, it meant a rapturous meeting with people from all parts of Poland.

When John Paul finally left Warsaw to fly westwards by helicopter to Gniezno, the ancient city from which Poland had emerged as a nation and embraced Christianity more than 1,000 years ago, it was to be greeted once more with flowers and cheers of enthusiasm.

On Monday, 4th June, the Pontiff journeyed to Czestochowa where, for three days, he stayed at Jasna Gora (Bright Mountain) monastery, Poland's most popular religious shrine.

The Pope stirred an outpouring of faith and affection that no political leader in the contemporary world could hope to inspire, let alone command. When he draws children to him, it is not the calculated action of one who desires to impress but rather one which is striking only for its obvious warmth.

At Czestochowa, where the famous painting of the Black Madonna is enshrined, the Pope led approximately half a million pilgrims in a carefully compiled consecration of Poland and the universal church to Mary, 'Queen of Poland'. The veneration of the Mother of God is deeply engraved upon the consciousness of the Polish people.

Outside the monastery of Jasna Gora, Pope John Paul II, accompanied by Cardinal Wyszinski, met with the same enraptured response. Many among the pilgrims remarked upon the fact that His Holiness seemed to convey an almost tangible sense of strength and joy; joy in adversities overcome, joy in being a Christian and joy in being human.

On the evening of the 6th June, the Pope returned to Kraków *left and above and below right*, the community he had served for twenty years as bishop and archbishop. Here he was greeted with special affection.

On the following day he paid an emotional visit to his home-town of Wadowice *above*, now proudly flying both the Polish and the Vatican flags. Then, from the site of many fond memories, the Pope made a sorrowful journey to the death-haunted railyards of Birkenau *below*.

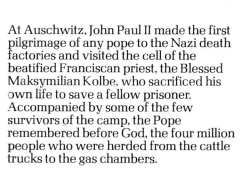

At Auschwitz, John Paul II made the first pilgrimage of any pope to the Nazi death factories and visited the cell of the beatified Franciscan priest, the Blessed Maksymilian Kolbe, who sacrificed his own life to save a fellow prisoner. Accompanied by some of the few survivors of the camp, the Pope remembered before God, the four million people who were herded from the cattle trucks to the gas chambers.

89

Possibly the most moving moment of the Pope's Polish visit was a Mass held among the barbed-wire fences, prison blocks and watch-towers of what he termed "a place built on hatred and contempt for man". To the hundreds of thousands among the congregation at this Mass, concelebrated by priests who had themselves been prisoners in the camp, Auschwitz must act as a reminder of the ultimate expression of human hatred. "It is necessary to think with fear of how far hatred can go, how far man's destruction of man can go, how far cruelty can go."

In preparation for the Pontiff's visit, the state had split the country into quadrants round Warsaw, Gniezno, Czestochowa and Kraków and citizens were directed to attend ceremonies only in their zone. Workers, students and schoolchildren were warned against absenting themselves during his stay. Yet despite such efforts and despite the failure of Polish television to show any sizeable crowds, the crowds were indisputably there.

93

By the time, on 10th June, the Pope's visit drew to its conclusion, his pilgrimage had been witnessed by an estimated 18 million people, leaving with them encouragement to challenge for freedom with all the strength of their Christian faith.
Below left: Pope John Paul II with Polish Communist Party Leader Edward Gierek.

On 29th September, Pope John Paul II once more ventured outside Italy, this time to undertake what in Italy, *La Stampa* described as "A trip to the edge of a volcano". The Pontiff's visit to Ireland was considered one of the most potentially explosive journeys ever to be undertaken by a pope. Yet John Paul remained undaunted. "Peace must be announced and proclaimed everywhere …It must be announced especially where it does not exist". As he told journalists who accompanied him during his flight, his mission was to be one of peace, of reconciliation and of prayer.

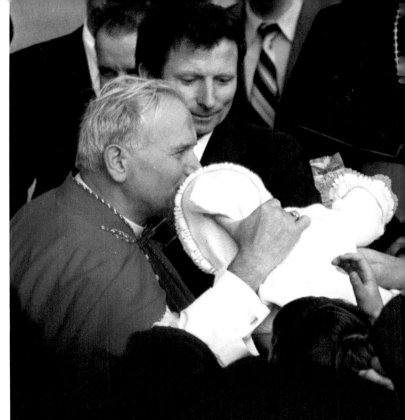

The reception at Dublin airport was possibly a little more restrained than that in, for example, Mexico City. The crowds of faithful were held at a distance by strict security controls. Nevertheless he was received with military honors and as the first reigning pontiff ever to visit Ireland stepped from his Aer Lingus Jumbo, St. Patrick, to be greeted by Cardinal Tonas O'Fiaich, Archbishop of Armagh, it was a moment of obvious joy and pride for the people of Ireland.

Ireland Welcomes Pope John Paul II

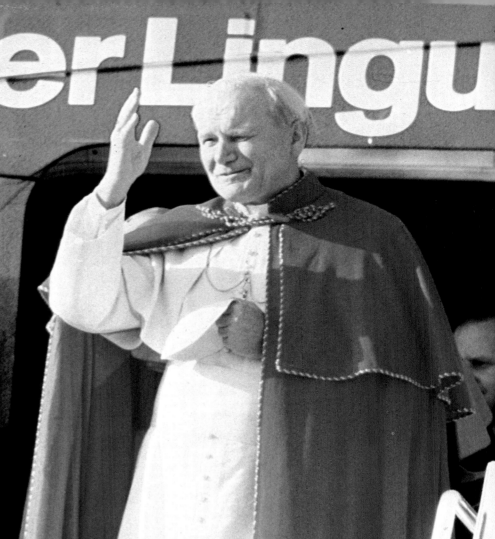

In Dublin's Phoenix Park, the Bishop of Rome and Pastor of the whole Roman Catholic Church joined in the celebration of the Eucharist with hundreds of thousands of Irish men and women. Calling to mind how many times across the centuries the Mass had been celebrated in this land, Pope John Paul urged for the continuance of acts of faith in these troubled times of prevailing materialism. "I am living a moment of intense emotion," he said; it was a moment shared by an immense crowd of people who had travelled from far and wide to catch a glimpse of their Holy Father.

Overleaf: In the celebrated 'Popemobile', the Pope made his way through a sea of waving flags and dancing and cheering people.

Joannes Paulus PP. II

1. X . 79 .

The crowds at Phoenix Park were an indication of the numbers and the atmosphere that were to follow the Pope throughout his three day visit to Ireland. Cheers, singing and a general air of festivity followed his repeated call for peace. "Peace cannot be established by violence; peace can never flourish in a climate of terror, intimidation and death" …"on my knees I beg you to turn away from the paths of violence and to return to the ways of peace."

Overleaf: Galway Racecourse was miraculously transformed by countless young people, assembled for a Pontifical Mass.

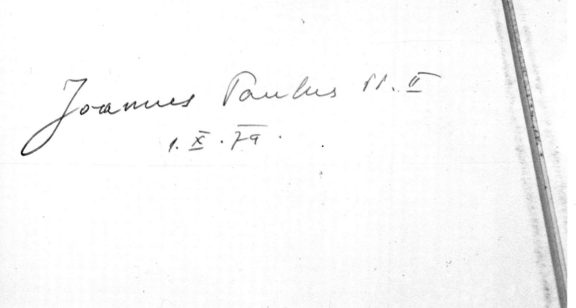

When John Paul II left Ireland, leaving behind him a vision of renewed hope, it was to fly directly to America. For the first time as Pope, he was visiting a country in which the majority of the population were not Roman Catholics but this did not appear to temper the warmth of his reception. At Logan International Airport, Rosalynn Carter, acting as her husband's personal emissary welcomed him with the words: "Americans of every faith have come to love you in a very special way," and the crowds straining to see him through the Boston rain added poignancy to her speech.

One of the primary objectives of the Pope's visit to America was to give an address to the United Nations Assembly. Having been warmly welcomed by Dr. Kurt Waldheim, the Secretary General, the Pope proceeded to deliver a speech lasting 61 minutes, which reflected a disconcertingly powerful intellect and which contained a defiant challenge to delegates of countries which still practice persecution in the name of security. John Paul's main theme was that peace is threatened by any violation of human rights anywhere, and that the U.N. can fulfil its peace-keeping mission only if it remembers and applies its own 1948 Universal Declaration of Human Rights.

A crowd of approximately 75,000 waited impatiently for the Pope in New York's Yankee Stadium and when he finally arrived in his white reconstructed Ford Bronco, the rhythmic clapping, and flashing of cameras, gave him the reception of a superstar. Yet his homily during the mass was to warn against the hedonistic values of the superstar culture, against what he described as "the frenzy of consumerism".

Overleaf: Undaunted by the weather, eager New Yorkers packed the streets for John Paul's motorcades.

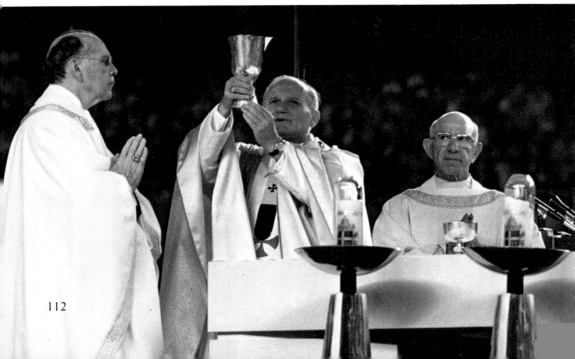

112

The Pope had come to America tired from
an emotional and demanding stay in Ireland.
Yet even at the point of exhaustion at the
end of each marathon day, he radiated
warmth, humor and strength. By the second
day in New York, he was visibly at his ease,
smiling and waving with delight en route to
a morning service at St. Patrick's Cathedral
and characteristically embracing any
children he encountered.

At Shea Stadium, 60,000 people were present for the Pope's final New York appearance. Despite the weather, they listened attentively to his words of farewell: "Above all, a city needs a soul if it is to become a true home for human beings. You, the people must give it soul, by loving each other."

In Philadelphia the Pope celebrated Mass for a huge and enthusiastic congregation in Logan Circle. It was in Philadelphia also that John Paul chose to make a direct and highly controversial pronouncement reaffirming traditional doctrine to 12,000 priests, nuns and seminarians in the Civic Center. Here the Pontiff insisted on the celibacy and the permanency of priesthood and rejected the idea of the ordination of women.

People came by every conceivable means of transport from throughout the Midwest and from as far away as Florida and New Mexico to wait for the Pontiff in a 600-acre expanse of farmland near Des Moines. On first hearing of the Pope's intended visit to America, Joe Hays, a local farmer, had written a note to invite John Paul to Iowa, and so, characteristically, the Pope had arranged to pause here in rural America.

In an address to an extraordinary convocation of 350 U.S. Roman Catholic Bishops in Chicago, the Pope issued the most unequivocal statement of his papacy on artificial contraception. He condemned both the ideology of contraception and contraceptive acts and went on to reiterate the Church's rejection of abortion, of divorce, of homosexual practice and of non-marital sex. Inevitably those who had hoped for more radical views were disappointed but amazingly, the cheering continued.

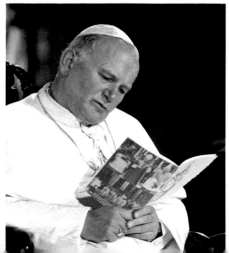

Pope John Paul II's visit to Washington and his meeting with President Carter were to mark the approaching conclusion of his stay. Throughout his visit he had extolled the freedom which America represented but together with his obvious affection for this land, there was also criticism. His traditional stance had raised many questions but perhaps the greatest mystery lay in the spectacle of countless Americans...Catholics and non-Catholics, religious and atheists.. applauding the Pope's attacks on consumerism. It was a tribute to the man and significantly, a tribute to values older than materialism.

First published in Great Britain 1979 by Colour Library International Ltd.
© 1979 Illustrations and text: Colour Library International Ltd., New Malden, Surrey, England.
Colour separations by FERCROM, Barcelona, Spain.
Display and text filmsetting by Focus Photoset, London, England.
Printed and bound by JISA-RIEUSSET, Barcelona, Spain.
All rights reserved.
ISBN 0 906558 29 8
COLOUR LIBRARY INTERNATIONAL.